LIGHT FROM WITHIN

LIGHT FROM WITHIN

Perspective on the biblical drama

by
MARGARET DEWEY

The Canterbury Press
Norwich

© Margaret Dewey 1993

First published 1993 by The Canterbury Press Norwich
(a publishing imprint of Hymns Ancient & Modern Limited,
a registered charity)
St Mary's Works, St Mary's Plain,
Norwich, Norfolk, NR3 3BH

*All rights reserved. No part of this publication which is copyright may
be reproduced, stored in a retrieval system, or transmitted, in any form
or by any means, electronic, mechanical, photocopying, recording, or
otherwise, without the prior permission of the publisher.*

Margaret Dewey has asserted her right under the
Copyright, Designs and Patents Act, 1988, to be identified
as Author of this Work

British Library Cataloguing in Publication Data

A catalogue record for this book is available
from the British Library

ISBN 1-85311-072-8

*Typeset by Datix International Limited
Bungay, Suffolk and
Printed and bound in Great Britain by
St Edmondsbury Press Limited
Bury St Edmunds, Suffolk*

The gifts he gave were that some would be apostles, some prophets, some evangelists, some pastors and teachers, to equip the saints for the work of ministry, for building up the body of Christ, until all of us come to the unity of the faith and of the knowledge of the Son of God, to maturity, to the measure of the full stature of Christ.

We must no longer be children, tossed to and fro by every wind of doctrine, by people's trickery, by their craftiness in deceitful scheming. But speaking the truth in love, we must grow up in every way into him who is the head, into Christ.

(Ephesians 4.11–15 NRSV)

FOREWORD

This book is the outcome of at least twenty-five years' reflection. It draws together, in a remarkable way, insights derived from several different fields, including Jungian psychology, the development of human personality, Christian spirituality and, above all, the story of God's dealings with his people from the slavery of Israel in Egypt to the coming of Christ and after.

The main theme is itself illuminating: that there is an analogy to be discovered between the stages of God's relations with his people as set out in the biblical story and the main phases of personal growth into maturity, through successive levels of consciousness.

The book will be of particular interest to clergy, ministers, theological students and those who work in the field of counselling, but anyone who is concerned with growth in discipleship and with mission will find much here to stimulate thought and action.

It is not always 'an easy read.' this is because the author moves freely within her different fields, and between the biblical text, the experience of the people of God in history, and the contemporary situation. But on the way there are frequent flashes of insight which, like lightning, illuminate whole areas of territory.

Margaret Dewey's work casts light on many matters of contemporary concern – the decade of evangelism, the relation between Christianity and other faiths, the Arab–Israeli conflict, the ordination of women (though we differ on this point) and the relation between personal prayer and the struggle for justice.

At the same time, we are allowed to enter to some degree into the author's own personal pilgrimage, and to appreciate the influence upon it of other writers (as diverse as Fr Herbert Kelly, Anthony Storr, William Johnston and Lesslie Newbigin) and of the societies in which she has lived and worked out her beliefs, including the Society of the Sacred Mission, the USPG, and St George's College, Jerusalem.

Easter 1993

DAVID P. WILCOX
Bishop of Dorking

CONTENTS

Foreword by the Bishop of Dorking	*page* vii
Acknowledgements	x
Introduction	xi
1. POETRY AND PARADOX	1
2. DISCIPLESHIP AND MISSION	6
3. THE GROWTH OF CONSCIOUSNESS	20
4. IN THE BEGINNING	30
5. EXODUS	39
6. THE ALL-PROVIDER	48
7. CONQUEST	61
8. THE PROMISED LAND	75
9. EXILE	91
10. DISPERSION	105
11. THE STONE THAT THE BUILDERS REJECTED	132
12. WHOLENESS	154
13. MISSION AND THE KINGDOM	163
Notes	177
Index	187

ACKNOWLEDGEMENTS

Except where otherwise indicated, scripture quotations are from the Revised Standard Version of the Bible, © 1946, 1952, 1971 by the Division of Christian Education of the National Council of Churches of Christ in the USA.

Grateful acknowledgement is made to authors and publishers for permission to quote from copyright material:
Darton, Longman & Todd Ltd for excerpts from *God of Surprises*, © 1985 by Gerard W. Hughes; *In Search of a Way*, © 1978 and 1986 by Gerard W. Hughes; *The Road to Daybreak*, © 1988 by Henri J. M. Nouwen; and *Community of Love*, © 1990 by the Executors of John Main;
William B. Eerdsman Publishing Co. for excerpts from *The Subversion of Christianity* by Jacques Ellul (1986) and *Foolishness to the Greeks* by Lesslie Newbigin (1986);
Faber & Faber Ltd for excerpts from *The Christian in Philosophy* by J. V. Langmead Casserley (1949) and *Education and the Modern Mind* by W. R. Niblett (1967);
Harper Collins Publishers Ltd for excerpts from *Christian Zen* by William Johnston, *The Mirrror Mind* by William Johnston, and *The Inner Eye of Love* by William Johnston, published by Harper Collins Publishers Ltd; and from *Surprised by Joy* by C. S. Lewis, originally published by Geoffrey Bles;
SCM Press Ltd for excerpts from *A Faith for This One World?* by Lesslie Newbigin (1961), *Honest Religion for Secular Man* by Lesslie Newbigin (1966), *The Finality of Christ* by Lesslie Newbigin (1969), *The Eternal Now* by Paul Tillich (1963), *Jews and Christians: The Myth of a Common Tradition*, by Jacob Neusner (1991), and *The Go-Between God* by John V. Taylor (1972);
SPCK for excerpts from *The Discovery of the Individual 1050-1200* © 1972 by Colin Morris, and from *Taking Hold of Change*, © 1975 by John Lawrence;
USPG for material used in the periodical *Thinking Mission* (1974-1988) and for an excerpt from the 1974 USPG annual report, *This World and the Next*, by Peter Wyld;
The World Council of Churches for excerpts from 'The Curative Community' by Erna Hoch, in *Man in Community*, © 1966 by the World Council of Churches.
Also from *The Transformation of Man*, © 1967 by Rosemary Haughton, published by Geoffrey Chapman. Reprinted by permission of Cassells plc;
Brighter Than a Thousand Suns by Robert Jungk, originally published in English by Victor Gollancz. Reprinted by permission of Scherz Verlag;
That Hideous Strength by C. S. Lewis, published 1945 by The Bodley Head. Reprinted by permission of Random House UK Ltd;
Contemplation in a World of Action by Thomas Merton, published 1971 by Allen & Unwin. Reprinted by permission of International Thomson Publishing Services Ltd;
Depth Psychology and a New Ethic, by Erich Neumann, © 1969 by Hodder & Stoughton Ltd and the C. G. Jung Foundation for Analytical Psychology. Reprinted by arrangement with Shambhala Publications, Inc., 300 Massachusetts Avenue, Boston, MA 02115;
The Origins and History of Consciousness by Erich Neumann, © 1954 by the Bollingen Foundation Inc., published by Princeton University Press. Reprinted by permission of Princeton University Press;
The Hidden Revolution, © 1978 by Ellis Rivkin, published by Abingdon Press. Reprinted by permission of Curtis Brown Ltd;
The Lost Tools of Learning by Dorothy L. Sayers, published by Methuen & Co. Ltd in 1948;
The Silicon Idol, © 1984 by Michale Shallis; reprinted by permission of Oxford University Press;
Sexual Deviation, © 1964 by Anthony Storr, published by Penguin Books Ltd Reprinted by permission of Peters, Fraser & Dunlop Ltd.
Who Needs the Church? © 1983 by Gerald Priestland, published by the St Andrew Press. Reprinted by permission of Sylvia Priestland.

The author has made every endeavour to trace and obtain permission for the use of copyright material, but in cases of oversight or error, offers sincere apologies and undertakes to acknowledge in a future edition.

INTRODUCTION

My basic outline, of the growth of consciousness in relation to the Bible and the experience of the people of God in history, is a working hypothesis which I hope may prove as suggestive and illuminating to others as it has been to me for a quarter of a century. It offers a new way of understanding the different stages in our discipleship, and imparts new urgency to the call (Ephesians 4.11–15) to grow up to full maturity in Christ.

While living in Australia in the early 1960s, I taught ascetical theology at Ridley College in Melbourne. After my return to England in 1963, it became increasingly clear that ascetical theology could no longer credibly be taught in the traditional way. This book is, in part, the outcome of that realisation. My outline first took shape in connection with some lectures given at Kelham Theological College in 1969 and 1970, at St Stephen's House in Oxford in 1971 and later (in different form) at Chichester Theological College and at Cuddesdon. Some of the material has been used in various forms in USPG's quarterly *Thinking Mission*, which it fell to me to produce for fifteen years in the 1970s and 1980s.

I am much indebted to the Society of the Sacred Mission, of one of whose priories I am a member, and to the United Society for the Propagation of the Gospel, with which I have been associated in one capacity or another since 1964. Among my long-suffering friends I owe special gratitude to Gilbert Russell for introducing me to depth psychology and the thinking of C. G. Jung, to the late Eric Symes Abbott for a quarter-century of friendship and encouragement, and to the late Gilbert Sinden SSM (for ten years Director of Studies at St George's College in Jerusalem) for many biblical and other insights. Gilbert Russell, Vincent Strudwick, Michael Wilson, Ian Jagger, Kennedy Thom, John Gowing, John Southgate and David Wilcox kindly read the draft manuscript at various stages and made many valuable suggestions; they are not, however, to be blamed for the shortcomings of the final version, responsibility for which is mine alone.

M.D.

Abbreviations:
- AV = Authorised Version
- CMS = Church Missionary Society
- JB = Jerusalem Bible
- NRSV = New Revised Standard Version
- RSV = Revised Standard Version
- RV = Revised Version
- SCM = Student Christian Movement
- SPCK = Society for the Promotion of Christian Knowledge
- SSM = Society of the Sacred Mission
- USPG = United Society for the Propagation of the Gospel
- WCC = World Council of Churches

I
Poetry and Paradox

In recent years it has been my privilege to spend a good deal of time (around three years, in all) at St George's College in Jerusalem, working in the College library, joining in College activities (including two memorable sojourns in the Sinai desert) and worshipping with the indigenous Arabic-speaking Christians, many of whose families have been witnessing there, where it all began, since the Day of Pentecost. Much of the time I shared a flat only yards from where the Mandelbaum Gate between east and west used to be. (I remember 'crossing over' there on a brief visit in 1960.) We looked across No Man's Land into the ultra-Orthodox Jewish Mea Shearim district, whence the warning Shabbat siren sounds every Friday, eighteen minutes before sundown. From a mosque just down the road, the muezzin issues the day's first call to prayer around 4 am, and at 6 am the great bell tolls from the Church of the Resurrection in the Old City.

Especially after the beginning of the Palestinian *intifada* or 'uprising' in the occupied territories in 1987, I became vividly aware of living in the midst of the biblical drama, which is still going on. There are soldiers everywhere in Bethlehem at Christmas—but so were there on the first Christmas, with the crowds there for the Roman census. There are soldiers everywhere in the Old City during Holy Week—but so were there at Passover-time two thousand years ago. The actors change; the plot remains the same. In that tiny strip of land (150 miles from Dan to Beersheba, fifty from the Mediterranean to the Dead Sea) Jacob and Esau still contend for their common homeland. And the great powers of the day have been fishing in those troubled waters at least since the days of Abraham. That land bridge where three continents meet is a crossroads of cultures: Jerusalem itself sits on top of the watershed, looking west into the settled civilisation of the Mediterranean, east into the desert. Medieval maps show Jerusalem as the centre of the world and in that ancient city, captured by David from the Jebusites three thousand years ago and sacred today to three religions, both the aspirations and the anguish of a sinful world are still focussed as by a burning-glass. One sees why it was *there* that redemption had to be wrought.

The 'Jerusalem experience' at St George's has profoundly influenced my thinking, as the Bible and its context have become living realities. But this book has its origin in two earlier 'disclosure experiences'.

The first occurred in 1951 in my first term at theological college. We had some lectures on normal developmental psychology, and in some of the descriptions of infants and small children I recognised with a shock a good bit of my own supposedly adult self. This led to my introduction to depth psychology, including a couple of years of analysis, and opened up a whole new dimension of discipleship.

The second 'disclosure experience' took place in 1967. I had been reading Sartre's little autobiography, *Words*, and I was sitting behind the choir in Westminster Abbey one Sunday morning. It was Septuagesima, and the first lesson was from Genesis 1: 'In the beginning God created the heaven and the earth. And the earth was without form, and void; and darkness was upon the face of the deep . . .' Suddenly it hit me like a brick between the eyes: the existentialist 'abyss of non-being'—those old Hebrews knew all about it! My mind whirled. Who wrote that? Somebody in the Exile. *Of course* they knew all about it!— the bottom had dropped out of their universe with the fall of Jerusalem. This sent me back to the Old Testament with new eyes.

The new eyes were partly provided by the late Erich Neumann's *The Origins and History of Consciousness*,[1] especially a luminous passage in which he observes that the coming of consciousness is the real point of creation mythology. Gabriel Hebert's invaluable little paperback *The Old Testament from Within*[2] was particularly helpful at this point. I came to see how the whole Bible, and especially the Old Testament, presents the archetypal saga of how God deals with people, individually and collectively, at different stages of their formation. My debt to Neumann is very great; and also to the missiological thinking of Lesslie Newbigin, who insists that what we are offered in the Christian faith is not something to be described as 'the best among the religions' but 'something which, if it is true, is the clue to all history—the history of the world, and the history of my own soul'.[3] Many others have illuminated my thinking over the years. If I have any claim to originality, it is in the overall framework and the juxtaposition within it of things usually considered in other contexts.

The thinking here, as in the Bible, is analogical rather than logical. (What are our Lord's parables but analogies?) It is less akin to the literal-minded intellectual, analytical 'left-hemisphere' thinking which modern Western education has emphasised than to the imaginative, intuitive 'right-hemisphere' thinking characteristic of traditional cultures, which think in metaphors and symbols, perceive patterns and relationships, and synthesise complementary parts into wholes. Jesus, as we see him in the gospels, is neither a systematic theologian nor a rabbinic interpreter of the Law, but one who communicates the deep things of his own soul to ours through metaphor and dramatic action. Metaphor is the primary language of theology; conceptual language is secondary.

Both kinds of thinking are needed if we are to be fully human, but concerning God and the things of God, poetry and paradox will take us further into the mystery than rationalist philosophy. This is true at all levels, from the 'way of paradox' taught by a learned mystic like Meister Eckhart[4] to the deceptive simplicity of a Christmas carol:

> O wonder of wonders, which none can unfold:
> The Ancient of Days is an hour or two old;

> The Maker of all things is made of the earth,
> Man is worshipped by angels, and God comes to birth.

This sort of approach to scripture is urged by William Johnston in his illuminating little paperback *Christian Zen*.⁵ He describes the *ko-an* or paradox on which some schools of Zen teach one to meditate (e.g. 'What is the sound of one hand clapping?'). The gospels, he says, abound in *koan*: 'Let the dead bury their dead'; 'He that loves his life will lose it'; 'This is my body'. One could say that 'Christianity is one tremendous *koan* that makes the mind boggle and gasp in astonishment; and faith is the breaking through into that deep realm of the soul which accepts paradox and mystery with humility'. Fr Johnston bids us use the scriptures as *koan*, to balance our academic approach. 'Put aside for a while your critical faculties of reasoning and arguing. Stop asking whether Jesus did or did not walk on the water, whether there was or was not a star to guide the Wise Men. Stop asking what it all means, because what it means if less important than what it does to you.' We need, he says, to let the words enter into us and live at the psychedelic level. This is how the gospel writers often use the Old Testament, and it is how mystics like St John of the Cross and St Bernard use the Bible: they speak from 'a realm that lies beyond and beneath the superficial discursiveness of the scholar'. Moreover, 'the men who wrote the Scriptures were operating at this level. They were *koan*-makers who did not write for scientists and did not want to be taken at the level of rationalisation alone'.

Jacques Ellul also insists on the essentially paradoxical nature of biblical revelation: 'We *never* find a single, logically connected truth followed by another truth deduced from it. There is no logic in the biblical revelation. There is no "either-or", only "both-and".'⁶ St Paul tells us we are saved by grace—yet we are to work out our own salvation. God is almighty—yet we are free; he is transcendent and unknowable—yet he enters history and is known and fully present in Jesus Christ. '*Everything* in the Bible is contradictory. Yet there is revelation only as the contradictions are held together.' This is also how the Talmud, that great storehouse of rabbinic wisdom, works: the basic text is in the middle of the page, surrounded by a number of different, sometimes apparently conflicting, rabbinic interpretations.

The Western mind is obsessed with unity, but the complementarity which can firmly grasp both halves of a paradox has proved to be the way of knowledge for modern physicists seeking to understand the material world (for example, how the mutually exclusive yet experimentally verified 'wave' and 'particle' theories of light can *both* be true). It was so for early Christian theologians seeking to reconcile their three-fold experience of God as Father, Son and Holy Spirit with their belief in one God, and their two-fold experience of Jesus as both God and man.[7] It can be so for us today, as we let the poetry and the paradox work within us.

2

Discipleship and Mission

The presuppositions of the Bible are set forth in narrative form in its preface, Genesis 1–11. The writing here is mythological. This does not mean that it is a fairy tale or untrue. On the contrary, it conveys the profoundest truths, relevant to every generation including our own.

Many Christians find the utterances of modern theologians about 'myth' in the Bible deeply disturbing. This kind of reaction means that myth and history are being understood as somehow mutually exclusive. In fact, myth is often metaphysics written as history, and a great deal of history is the acting out of collective myths. Narrative is the most natural way of doing philosophy or theology in Hebrew, which is an exceedingly concrete and personal language. (There is no neuter gender in Hebrew: nothing is an 'it'; even inanimate objects and abstract ideas are either masculine or feminine.) But this in no way precludes the possibility that a myth may become earthed in history.[1]

'Myth, far from being childish nonsense, is an essential ingredient in human psychological life,' says William Johnston, echoing Jung. 'Human beings need myth and story no less than they need bread and rice. Without the great symbols provided by the holy books, men and women are like lost children; they are left without meaning, they are wandering in the dark.' All the great religions 'are telling us a story or stories that will nourish our unconscious, live in our archetypes, answer our deeper questions, give meaning to the riddle of life.' But Judaism and Christianity go further: they claim,

> that their holy books are not only myth but also history. Jews and Christians believe that God really chose a people

and that he spoke through Abraham and Isaac and Jacob and the prophets. Obviously this does not mean that the Bible can be called critical history in our modern sense of this term. We know that it contains legend and poetry and fiction. But it does mean that the Bible recounts *saving events* and that the words describe and explain these events.[2]

The editors of Genesis, looking back over their own catastrophic experience with the hindsight of exiles and the insight of the prophets, ask the devastating question: 'Adam, where art thou?' Adam is Everyman—you and me.[3]

'In the beginning, God': this is the first presupposition of the Bible. Like all presuppositions, including those of modern science, it cannot be proven but only taken for granted as a working hypothesis.[4] (William Temple, following Pascal, used to say 'faith is betting your life that there *is* a God'.) The Hebrew *rōsh* and its Greek equivalent *archē* mean both 'the beginning' (in time) and also the foundation, source or fountainhead. The biblical doctrine of creation is less concerned with whether the universe did or did not begin with a 'big bang' than with the on-going relatedness of all created things to the Creator.

This in no way conflicts with the findings of modern science.[5] The 'solid matter' of Newton's mechanical physics has turned out to be minute electrical charges rushing about in otherwise empty space; its observable properties are illusions of our perception; its stability, a mystery. As the physicist Fritjof Capra observes, 'at the subatomic level the interrelations and interactions between the parts of the whole are more fundamental than the parts themselves. There is motion, but there are, ultimately, no moving objects; there is activity, but there are no actors; there are no dancers, there is only the dance.'[6] Physicists now see the universe as a web of relationships which include the human observer: the subject/object dichotomy loses its meaning and there is no such thing as an 'objective fact'. The doctrine of the Trinity tells us that there is relatedness at the heart of God. It may even be that, in a profound sense, God *is* the relatedness between the Persons, for we are told that God is love (1 John 4.16).⁷

Try meditating imaginatively on the possibility of a power cut in the universe: there really is darkness on the face of the deep. At the bottom of everything, *God* (say the editors of Genesis)—and without God, no bottom to anything, for things exist only in their relatedness to God. But with God, creation: 'God said . . . and it was so.'

So the Christian takes matter seriously, for God takes it seriously enough to have become incarnate in it, and his redemptive purpose includes the whole created cosmos, culminating in the 'new heaven and new earth' announced in Isaiah 65.17 and referred to in Revelation 21.1 and 2 Peter 3.13.⁸

God is real and not just a name for our ideas: *God acts*: the initiative is always his. This is the burden of the 'gospel of God' proclaimed throughout his long life by Father Herbert Kelly of Kelham. In a little booklet on 'The Use of the Old Testament', written in Japan in 1914, he observed that,

> there is no book of any other religion in the whole world in which God is so trenchantly real, in which He is such a tremendous actuality, to be reckoned with in every moment of life. All through the Old Testament, God is set forth and spoken of as the Creator and actual Ruler of heaven and earth. Whether men know God or not, through men or without men, all things come to pass according to His will . . . In the Old Testament, God is not an ideal, nor a symbolical expression of human thought, but a reality Who acts whether men think of Him or not.

The corollary to belief in one Creator God is mission to the nations: 'Turn to me and be saved, all the ends of the earth: for I am God, *and there is no other*' (Isaiah 45.22). No more tribal gods: the one transcendent God is indeed concerned with us, but he is equally concerned with all other peoples. Here is the end of ethnic self-sufficiency and the mainspring of mission: 'It is too light a thing that you should be my servant to raise up the tribes of Jacob and to restore the preserved of Israel; I will give you as a light to the nations, that my salvation may reach to the ends of the earth' (Isaiah 49.6).

Such is the gospel according to Second Isaiah.[9] (Who knows? he may have been one of the editors of Genesis, who reshaped Middle Eastern creation myths into a vehicle for their own monotheistic metaphysics.) It leads away from tribalism ('We have Abraham to our father') to the discovery of Adam and the kinship of the whole human race,[10] both in our common calling and in the fateful ambiguity of our human nature.

Adam is given responsibility: he is to share the creative miracle of speech, and he is given pastoral oversight[11] over the rest of God's creation. But as soon as he starts gardening, the simplicity of his paradisal world is invaded by doubt, and ambition, and the anxiety of choice.

Adam gets into trouble because he can't say 'No', when he ought to, to something in itself good. Fertility is good, but unlimited population growth guarantees less-than-human life for most of those born. Productivity is good, but unlimited economic growth becomes a cancer devouring the earth. Technological achievement is good, but if its blind momentum is not checked by a deliberate human 'No', it becomes a Moloch demanding human sacrifice.

Adam discovers the ambiguity of creation, good-*and*-evil, through his own experience ('Thy right hand shall teach thee terrible things!'—Psalm 45.4 AV). *God* sees his creation and sees that it is good. But to our finite eyes in a three-dimensional universe, all created things, seen in the light, cast shadows. This poses Adam a problem: what to do with the shadow? Once aware of good *and* evil in all creation (including himself), can he accept ambiguity as a fact of life in its wholeness?

He does finally acknowledge his nakedness, but refuses to accept responsibility for his own actions. Seeing himself as an injured innocent, he projects the blame onto somebody else, so that instead of wholeness there is polarisation into opposites.

Individuals and communities have been doing it ever since, for polarisation and projection constitute an essential stage in our coming to consciousness. The scapegoat (Leviticus 16.20–22 AV) is a psychological necessity for those at this stage: the dark, disturbing aspects of human nature (those which clash with our current ideal of perfection (*must* be unloaded somewhere—onto enemies, aliens, outcasts, untouchables, social lepers or the structures of society—until we attain a maturity secure enough for us to withdraw our projections, acknowledge our own shadow, and accept ambiguity as an integral part of God's creation.

Communities think in absolutes. The communal world is safely classified into Goodies and Baddies. Cultural diversity is unacceptable. Morality is self-evident ('natural law') and all deviant behaviour culpable. Communal presuppositions may not be questioned; there must be certainty. (Hence one-party states: the British parliamentary concept of HM *Loyal* Opposition is very sophisticated indeed. It presupposes in its practitioners an individuality which can welcome diversity without feeling threatened.) Communal justice is strict, an eye for an eye. Good must be seen to triumph, evil to be punished—and there is not the slightest doubt which is which. It is the morality of those self-righteous psalms, sure of their own innocence and of the iniquity of their foes.

The conversion of St Paul stands for all time as a warning that certainty can be mistaken. If we both hold on to our integrity and also keep on growing, sooner or later our notions of right and wrong must change.

The reason why it is so difficult to love our neighbour as ourself is that there is so much of ourself we don't love and fear to acknowledge. We have first to learn to love the enemy within. Meanwhile, it is less disturbing to see the mote in our neighbour's eye than the beam in our own. *There is nothing the human race fears so much as self-knowledge.* This is the real point of Oedipus myth, usually overlooked in the Freudian interpretation. In the ancient Greek myth Oedipus, exposed in infancy but found and brought up by foster parents in ignorance of his true parentage, later unwittingly kills his father in a chance encounter and subsequently marries his mother; discovering the truth years later, he puts out his own eyes rather than look upon the consequences of his own action. Freud used the term 'Oedipus complex' for the (repressed, unconscious) sexual attraction of a boy toward his mother and his consequent (unconscious) desire to murder his father. But the real point of the myth is not *what* Oedipus refused to see but *that* he refused to see.

Adam passes the buck to Eve; Eve passes it to the serpent.

So God tells them the blunt truth: human life is full of sorrow and suffering and death. What the earth brings forth spontaneously is thorns and thistles, and to make it grow anything else will cost Adam hard work. Eve, who wanted everything that was going, will get the lot.

Not even family life is free from ambiguity—not even the brotherhood of man. Cain's anxiety over his own non-acceptance turns into envy and aggression and he is unable to say 'No' to his murderous impulse.

The lesson of Genesis 1–11 is that *most folk, given freedom, will misuse it*. The gravitational pull back into the irresponsible self-centredness of infancy is too powerful for us to overcome by moral effort alone. This universal human predicament theologians call 'original sin', which has been described as 'the one theological doctrine for which there is empirical evidence'.[12]

Of course not all accept the evidence. Pelagius in the fifth century did not, and Pelagianism remains the most characteristic British heresy. Muslims do not, and hence see no need for a saviour. Modern Judaism has no doctrine of original sin, but the ancient Hebrews understood it well enough. 'The heart of man is deceitful above all things, and desperately corrupt,' says Jeremiah (17.9), echoing the references in Genesis 6.5 and 8.21 to the *yetzer ha'ra* or 'evil imagination' of the human race. After years of strict observance as an Orthodox Jew, Paul the Pharisee is reduced to near-despair at the futility of moral effort as a way of self-perfection:

> I do not understand my actions. For I do not do what I want, but I do the very thing I hate. . . . I can will what is right, but I cannot do it. For I do not do the good I want, but the evil I do not want is what I do. . . . Wretched man that I am! Who will deliver me from this body of death? (Romans 7.15–24)

God's answer to the human predicament, as Paul has thankfully discovered, is given to us in Christ.

The human solution, pressed upon us by all revolutionaries, is to sweep away both the wicked oppressors and the corrupt structures of society and to make a new start. But God thought of that first, and it doesn't work. It is *after* the slate has been wiped clean by the Flood and a new start made with righteous Noah that we read of the Tower of Babel—a notable essay in human cooperation and technology. Alas, that monumental symbol of human arrogance leads not to heaven (as in the utopian plan) but to the breakdown of communication and a fragmentation of mankind not to be reversed till Pentecost.

The rest of the Bible, from Genesis 12 to Revelation, demonstrates God's strategy for dealing with the awkward facts. God will not revoke human freedom (as men are wont to do), not even if they use it to crucify his Son . . . or each other. Rather, *God will save the faithless many by the faithful few who freely respond.* It is the only way of salvation for *all* which does not take away from some the freedom that makes us human.

The Cross is the shadow cast by human freedom. There is nothing whatever in the Bible to suggest that in this life all men ever will freely respond to God. On the contrary, very many will prefer darkness to light, right up to that apocalyptic moment when 'every eye *shall see*'—whether they like it or not.

Mission is at the heart of Christian discipleship: 'As my Father has sent me, even so I send you' (John 20.21). And discipleship is prerequisite to mission, for the mission is not ours but God's. The implementing of God's mission in human history begins with the call of Abraham (in whose seed all nations of the earth are to be blessed) to go out from his own land and people, putting his trust in God alone. Abraham is the archetypal pilgrim on the Way. Too many of us, like so many of those who visit the Holy Land today, are content to be not pilgrims but tourists.

Authentic Christianity on the New Testament pattern (as taught, for example, in the Sermon on the Mount) is possible only in relatively small communities of the mature and committed. 'Jesus told his disciples that they were a little flock,' says Jacques Ellul in *The Subversion of Christianity*.[13] 'All his comparisons tend to show that the disciples will necessarily be small in number and weak. ... Jesus does not seem to have had a vision of a triumphant and triumphal church encircling the globe. He always depicts for us a secret force that modifies things from within.'

But in the days of Constantine, the Church's very success transformed it from a fellowship of the Spirit into an established institution with a priestly hierarchy. In becoming a state religion, Christianity ceased to be a faith and became an ideology with a moral code. This was not necessarily a bad thing, for states need an ideology if they are to cohere, but it is not the gospel. As Ellul observes, to most folk the ongoing relationship with a loving God which the gospel offers is not good news. Most prefer the certainty of law to the unpredictable generosity of grace and the risks of freedom and responsibility.

The tension between the 'little flock' and the needs of society at large was one of the factors that led to the rise of monasticism. That tension is still with us. Jesus warns us that strait is the gate and narrow the way that leads to life, and few there be that find it (Matthew 7.14). But God's offer, of fellowship with him and sharing in his mission, is to be made known to all. All are to be given the chance to know his love, and to respond.

* * *

Such is the theology of mission. But there are many obstacles.

The earliest Christian creed is 'Jesus is Lord'. The Easter victory reaches its climax in the Ascensiontide celebration of the enthronement of Christ as King. The Pentecostal outpouring of the Holy Spirit then empowers Christians to be his witnesses to the ends of the earth, inviting all to accept Jesus as Saviour and Lord.

This means change. There is today, rightly, much concern among Christians to find effective means of communication. But we must not assume that if only the gospel is understood, all will flock to accept it. The enthronement of Christ involves the dethronement of all other gods. The more clearly the relevance of Christ to things-as-they-are is seen, the more resistance is evoked. This is the judgement: light comes into the world, *and men prefer darkness* (John 3.19). Out of his own experience Jesus warns that the good seed of the Word of God will fall on stony ground and among thorns as well as on good ground (Matt. 13.1–9). The opening of the eyes of the blind is the first of the messianic signs (Isaiah 35.5), and men crucified the Messiah. Jesus warns us to expect persecution if we are true to him; it is false prophets of whom all speak well. We are not called to success, but to faithfulness. Results are God's affair.

In the earliest preaching of the gospel, Peter in Jerusalem (Acts 2.14–36) and Paul at Antioch in Asia Minor (Acts 13.16–41) both speak to Jews and to non-Jewish 'God-fearers' who attend the synagogue and whose familiarity with Jewish experience of God-in-history can be taken for granted. It is instructive to compare this full gospel of redemption with Paul's groping after something that might be grasped either by simple pagans at Lystra, whose reaction to his ministry of healing has been to take him and

Barnabas for gods of the pagan sort and to try to worship *them* (Acts 14.8–18) or by sophisticated Athenian sceptics (Acts 17.16–31). Both these groups lack the 'Old Testament' preparation of Jew and God-fearer.

Today in the West we are less often in the position of Peter at Pentecost or Paul in the synagogue than of Paul at Lystra or Athens. We can take *nothing* for granted.

The New Testament takes for granted certain assumptions which were first articulated by the Hebrew prophets, then hammered into Jewish consciousness by the experience of exile and dispersion. Muslims (those other children of Abraham) share some of them, but probably two-thirds of the world's population do not. Today even in the Western heartlands of what was once Christendom there is a massive regression from them:

(a) From a sense of history—that is, from time experienced as going from somewhere to somewhere, with meaning and purpose. Without a sense of history, the present moment is no longer seen in meaningful context. And meaninglessness is the deepest malaise of modern Western civilisation. It is not of course a peculiarly modern malaise, as the Book of Ecclesiastes makes clear.

(b) From acknowledgement of one God who is transcendent to his creation (as a Creator, Saviour and Judge must be) as well as immanent within it—and therefore also from belief in creation, salvation, and judgement.

(c) From personal responsibility, announced by Jeremiah (31.29–34) as the content of the New Covenant in which each individual, no longer wholly dependent on communal tradition *about* God, has direct personal knowledge *of* him and responsibility to him.

(d) From understanding that even innocent suffering can be redemptively used. The Bible makes clear that sin, not suffering, is the worst evil.

(e) From rationality and the creative word. The disintegration of language in our time is a particularly disturbing regression from full humanity. ('In the beginning was the Word,' says St John, and it is quite literally true of our coming to consciousness in infancy.) Grammar, once the only training in logic which most people received, is no longer taught in many schools. The mass media reinforce a preference for images which simply impose themselves and discourage critical discourse. Television trivialises everything it touches, turning even human tragedy and natural disaster into entertainment, shortening our attention span and interrupting even serious programmes with commercials.[14] A distinguished Muslim scholar living in Britain has shrewdly observed that what characterises the modern secular world is not atheism but lack of spiritual seriousness.[15] It could be that this is the greatest of all obstacles to the gospel.

Addiction to television and video—and the medium *is* addictive—is particularly damaging to young children. Regardless of content, the medium itself blurs the distinction between fact and fantasy. It reduces viewers to passivity and stunts their capacity for conversation and rational thought, for real relationships with real people and for participation in the real world. The image comes to seem more real than the real world. This tendency is reinforced by the use of computers from primary school onward: both technologies redefine the world in unreal terms, as images on a screen.

The computer is a marvellous tool for tasks for which it is appropriate. Its unimaginable speed of calculation and the sheer quantity of information it can store make possible the wonders of space technology and many advanced techniques of medical treatment (and also the sophistication of modern weapons of mass destruction). But its model of reality excludes questions of value, emotion, personal experience and relationship, quality and purpose—the very things that make human life human, and which enable us to decide our priorities wisely.[16] In what is rightly called 'information technology', meaning is all too easily reduced to the transmission of information. And no amount of information can give us wisdom.

Already in the nineteenth century F. D. Maurice was

warning that our industrial society was inadvertently creating a kind of man to whom the gospel cannot be preached. Today no small part of the preparation for the gospel which took place in ancient Israel is being deliberately undone by a dominant culture vigorously promoted by the political and commercial principalities and powers of our technological society. There is thus much pre-evangelism to be done. No small part of our missionary task is (like John the Baptist) to prepare the way of the Lord. For us, too, this means challenging much that is taken for granted by our contemporaries.

* * *

It is sometimes suggested that other religions may provide for their adherents an alternative preparation for the gospel: that there may be (as it were) other Old Testaments. (This was first suggested by Clement of Alexandria around AD 200 with reference to Greek philosophy.) There is much truth in this, and faithful adherents of other faiths often put us to shame by their devotion and the quality of their life. It is also true that we may have something to learn from them about the fullness of Christ: can we really presume to think that we already know all there is to know about Christ, or equate our own grasp of truth with the truth itself? Jesus himself warns his disciples that 'I have yet many things to say to you, but you cannot bear them now' (John 16.12). Why should we suppose that he is only able to teach us through other Christians?

Nevertheless, I believe that it is according to the biblical pattern that God works out his purpose among all peoples. (The late Walbert Bühlmann, a distinguished Roman Catholic missionary and theologian, expounds this theme in *The Chosen Peoples*.[17]) The story of the Incarnation (what Bühlmann calls 'God's total self-communication in Jesus') at a particular time and place in history, and of God's long preparation of a people for it, does constitute a 'norm'—though our understanding of that story and its implications may be greatly enriched through the insights of those of other faiths.

So as a preparation for the gospel it needs to be asked, in each case, to what extent that particular faith does in fact teach you to take for granted what the New Testament takes for granted. Hindu and Buddhist attitudes to history, to the material universe and to human personality are very different from those taken for granted in the Bible and virtually exclude the possibility of a unique Incarnation. Buddhism assumes that suffering (not sin) is the worst evil, from which we should seek to escape. Islam denies original sin and hence any need for salvation, and says that Jesus did not die on the cross but was rescued by God at the last moment and taken to heaven.

But there is evidence to suggest that God is at work today *within* other faiths. Speaking at a USPG council meeting in 1987, Roger Hooker, for many years a CMS missionary in India, asked 'Why is it that twentieth-century biographies of the Prophet Muhammad portray him in more Christlike ways than earlier works? What do we make of the fact that more books about Jesus have been written by Jews in the last twenty or thirty years than in the whole of the previous two thousand? What do we say theologically about the enormous number of Hindus in India who now say they worship only Jesus—though of course they have not asked for baptism and are most unlikely to do so?'

Surely this is what we should expect if with St Paul we believe that it is in Christ that *all* things are created and sustained, and in and through him that all things (including all peoples and cultures) are to be gathered into one (Colossians 1.15–20, Ephesians 1.9–10). There is no place on earth to which *we* can *take* Christ (though we may bring an awareness of him), for there is no place where he is not already present and at work.

'Baptism in the church does not first and foremost mean salvation,' says Bühlmann. 'The unbaptised can be saved. Baptism in the church means, first and foremost, that we are called to be a part of the church's sacramental witness—to be witnesses to the fact that forgiveness of sins is announced in Jesus's name to all peoples (Luke 24.47ff).'[18] Conversion does not happen by our evangelistic efforts. It is the work of God. 'No one can come to me unless the Father who sent me draws him,' says Jesus (John 6.44), to which St Paul adds that 'no one can say "Jesus is Lord" except by the Holy Spirit' (1 Cor. 12.3). It was so understood from the very beginning: '*The Lord increased the number of those being saved*' (Acts 2.47).

All theology is done in particular contexts: there is no 'pure gospel' free of any cultural taint. But there is a very fine line between contextual theology and syncretism. There are those who now think that the harmonisation of the Christian faith with Greek philosophy, begun by Clement and others in Alexandria, has proved a mixed blessing. Medieval Christendom approximated more nearly to a mirror image of Islam than to the New Testament picture of the church.[19] And Western Christianity is today in an advanced state of syncretism with the secular world.

If we Gentiles would have the mind of Christ, we must get inside the drama of Israel's formation, for it is our own, *and it is still going on.* Their story is our story; it is the story of my life, and of yours.

3
The Growth of Consciousness

The Bible makes clear that God's mission takes different forms to people at different stages. The New Testament gospel cannot be proclaimed to Israel in Egypt: more than a thousand years of experience are needed before the Incarnation can meaningfully take place among them.

To the cheap labour at the bottom of Pharoah's affluent society God sends Moses (who has himself dropped out from the corridors of power) to lead, not a revolution, but an Exodus into the wilderness. During their Long March, Moses tells the mixed multitude who have come out of Egypt (Exodus 12.38) who they are and where they are going: he gives them identity and purpose, forming them into a people through the discipline of the Covenant relationship, feeding them with manna and the Word and with signs and wonders. The fastest-growing Christianity today is that which offers just such a formative experience—of a morally disciplined closed community gathered around a charismatic leader—to the rootless, the dispossessed, the detribalised, the alienated, the oppressed.

Those who seek an earthly Promised Land need a Joshua who will consecrate their aggressive energies in a holy war in which their own identity can be asserted over against the 'enemies of God'. A Joshua who refuses to be drawn into a violent liberation movement has, as yet, no place in their world.[1] At any given moment in history, very many are still at an Old Testament stage. This is the homeland of politically oriented liberation theologies. The liberation from sin which Jesus offers (Matthew 1.21) makes sense only after one has emerged from the collective consciousness of childhood into an adult capacity for personal responsibility.

To the heirs of David and of Solomon and his glory (the models for Christian kingship from Constantine to the British Empire) God sends prophets to point out the oppressive cost to others of their affluence. The prophets do not call upon the oppressed to revolt, but warn the oppressors what must inexorably follow if they do not repent and do justice:[2] 'election' is meant for responsibility and service, not for selfish privilege. When we read the prophet's call in Isaiah 6, we usually stop at verse 8, omitting the grim warning of verses 9–10. But it is these latter verses that are quoted or alluded to by all four evangelists and by St Paul.[3] Jeremiah and Ezekiel, too, are aware that God's word will be heeded only by a faithful remnant.[4]

To exiles dispersed in alien lands, and to those who return to a Jerusalem subject to pagan empires, God sends scribes to record his mighty acts in history and his will as understood in the Law, prophets to warn and to discern the meaning and redemptive use of suffering, poets and sages to utter wisdom, rabbis to teach the Way of discipleship. Jesus is recognised by his contemporaries as a prophet and a rabbi.

* * *

In embryology we learn that in the womb each of us climbs the ladder of physical evolution for himself. There was a time when you and I had gills like a fish; each of us starts life as a single cell, like an amoeba. Millions of years of evolution are foreshortened into nine months, but we cannot skip stages: each one of us experiences them all.

There is also a ladder of psychic evolution which each individual is called to climb in pursuit of the 'full-grown manhood' of which Ephesians 4.13 speaks. Our Lord himself *grew* to that stature (Israel as a nation, too—or at least a faithful remnant): for him, too, human life began in the womb of a mother and developed through birth, infancy, weaning, childhood and adolescence to maturity; and he, too, passed through the grave and gate of death. This gives an added dimension to the 'imitation of Christ' and to his call, 'Follow me'.

In the course of its own development, 'the individual ego consciousness has to pass through the same archetypal stages which determined the evolution of consciousness in the life of humanity,' observes Erich Neumann. 'The individual has in his own life to follow the road that humanity has trod before him, leaving traces of its journey in the archetypal sequence of the mythological images.'[5] In *The Origins and History of Consciousness*, this Jewish Jungian analyst explores the evolution of these archetypal images in Greek mythology from the matriarchal world of the Great Mother and the chthonic deities of the unconscious underworld to the conscious patriarchal world of Mt Olympus and the Age of Heroes. In so doing he incidentally sheds a flood of light on Christian discipleship.

In its reaction against paganism, official Judaism has understandably tried to suppress the mythologising tendency of the unconscious and to stress rational consciousness and morality. That tendency reasserted itself in the Middle Ages in the mysticism of the Kabbalah. (The Kabbalah surfaced again in Eastern European Jewry two centuries ago in Hasidism, the movement which inspired Martin Buber, by whom Neumann himself was much influenced.) In the Gentile world, esoteric movements from ancient Gnosticism to modern theosophy represent the same mythologising tendency of the unconscious. Very real perils lurk in these depths, and from New Testament times (e.g. 1 Tim. 6.20–21) onward, the Church has wisely discouraged such regressions into paganism. But understood simply as manifestations of depth psychology, such phenomena can yield valuable insights.

We become human through experience of personal relationship. Mature human personality has many layers, laid down in different kinds of relationship at different stages. There is a rhythm in this growth: first, integration into the environment, which nourishes us up to a certain point, then detachment from it when we are ready to move on: first *formation*, then *trans*formation.

'The ideal of the formation of man,' says Rosemary Haughton in *The Transformation of Man*,[6]

> is the process of using all the influences of culture—family affection, humane educational and political and social structures, and all the scientific know-how available—to help people to understand themselves and each other and the world they share, to adjust themselves to both without either undue aggressiveness or frightened conformity, and so to form satisfying and stable emotional and social relationships.

Life in a community in which mutual responsibility and care of the weak are taken for granted should, ideally, produce whole human beings. 'Nobody expects perfection in practice, but it is an imaginable ideal'—a kind of spiritual evolution.

The idea of transformation, on the other hand, 'is not imaginable at all, which is why we tend to place transformed man in a separate "place" called heaven'. Transformation represents not evolution but revolution.

> It begins with repentance—the rejection, along with actual sins, of the whole apparatus of natural virtue as irrelevant and misleading—and proceeds eventually to the desired dissolution of all that ordinary people value in themselves and others. The result of this dissolution, this death of the natural man, is the birth of the whole human being, the perfection of man, meaning both man as an individual and man as a race, because the process is at once personal and communal. And it takes place in Christ and nowhere else. It is what Christians call the resurrection, or eternal life.

Until recently the Catholic tradition of Christianity seemed mainly concerned with formation; the Reformed tradition, with transformation. Today, however, right across the ecclesiastical spectrum, 'the contradiction between man formed and man transformed is splitting the Christian consciousness at every level of community and personal life, and you *can't* adapt structures in such a way as to accommodate both, because structures are concerned solely with formation'. Transformation, on the other hand, happens in the gaps between the structures, or where structures are breaking down, or right outside them—in the wilderness. 'As long as "the world" is functioning efficiently, the word of power is unheard, or if it is heard it is a scandal, a threat, an offence, to be removed as quickly as possible.' But transformation does not happen without previous experience of structured life.

> 'The wilderness' as an idea presupposes the life of the man-ordered city and arable land. If all were wilderness there would be no word to distinguish it. And the idea of 'in-between' implies that there is a firm and enduring structure of life on either side of it, something for it to be 'between'. It is in the breaking down of the Law that the Spirit's work becomes apparent, but there has to be a Law to break down.

The Law is our schoolmaster to bring us to Christ (Galatians 3.24) and though both here and in the Epistle to the Romans Paul is trying to wean Jewish Christians from their reliance on law, he nowhere suggests that it might have been better if they had never known that formative discipline.

For pilgrims on the Way, transformation is not a once-for-all event but part of the alternating rhythm of growth. The exhilarating experience of 'conversion' can happen at any of the transformation-points in our pilgrimage, and it is tempting to try to perpetuate the exuberant joy and certainty which go with it. Peter wanted to stay on the Mount of Transfiguration (Mark 9.5). But we cannot stay permanently on the mountain-top. If we are to keep on growing, we must come down from our spiritual 'high' and assimilate our new vision and understanding into a new integration. All else apart, certainty is not the same as faith, and feelings can be very ambivalent: one wonders (for example) how the charismatics will cope with the Dark Night of the Soul. Theirs is a spirituality for beginnings, and new beginnings, where its power to transform is unquestioned, but the long, weary trek through the desert requires a different kind of sustenance.

Each new integration is at a new level of consciousness and (as we shall see) introduces a new way of experiencing identity and of relating to other people and to God. Each tends to evolve a theology and spirituality appropriate to that stage and which, to those within that stage, *seems* universally valid. This is the natural experience underlying denominationalism, class consciousness, and many other cultural phenomena, including differing views of morality and political theory. At any given moment in any given society, many levels of consciousness are represented, but one level predominates and sets the tone of the dominant culture, from which those at different stages of growth may feel alienated.

We cannot skip stages, though for adult disciples their duration may be greatly foreshortened.

Earlier levels are never wholly left behind: they persist, below our normal threshold of perception. Whether we like it or not, they continue powerfully to influence our thinking and feeling, our perception and action, and our prayer. Mostly we don't like it at all, and our unconscious will do almost anything to prevent such embarrassing self-knowledge from breaking through into consciousness. Freud is right about the mechanism of repression; it is not, however, only sexual and aggressive impulses that are repressed, but anything which clashes with our current world-view and lifestyle.

There is a tidal ebb and flow between the evolutionary surge upward onto the 'dry land' of consciousness and the undertow of entropy which will drag us back into the unconscious depths if we do not scramble to our feet in time. This is the basic human choice: to keep on growing and face the cost, or to give up the effort and slip back into apathy. Sin is persistence in, or regression to, attitudes and behaviour which are appropriate (or at least innocent) in earlier stages, especially infancy: we alienate ourselves from God by clinging to infantilism and childishness and refusing to grow up into the fullness of life in Christ to which he calls us (Ephesians 4.11–16).[7]

Sin is sometimes thought of as yielding to 'animal' impulses, e.g. people speak disparagingly of 'Nature red in tooth and claw' or of 'barnyard morals'. But no other species preys upon its *own kind* as we do, and barnyard animals are by definition those domesticated by man and kept under highly unnatural conditions. In the wild, sexual promiscuity is by no means the rule among the higher animals (birds and mammals): many are faithful to one mate for the whole of the time it takes to raise a brood of young (and some mate for life); with others, the male establishes by ritual combat his exclusive right to his 'harem'. We human beings, in gaining the capacity for rational control, have lost the instinctive controls which keep other animals' impulses within safe bounds. Hence what we regress to when we sin is not the instinctive behaviour of adult wild animals but the wholly unregulated behaviour of human infants, who have neither instinctive restraints nor (as yet) rational control.

We all have bits of unfinished business buried somewhere, transformations we didn't quite manage at the time, where emotional energy has got dammed up. Part of our personality makes the grade and establishes a workable lifestyle at the new level, but some energy has to be diverted to sentry duty to keep the unresolved problem below from unduly disturbing the present. We feel the pressure, but can normally cope in the relative calm of the new integration.

If and when anything threatens that, the new insecurity may awaken too many echoes below for comfort. If the buried problem is really serious, neurotic or psychotic symptoms may appear, or we may feel a generalised anxiety or depression with no visible cause proportionate to its intensity. External pressures may precipitate a break-down. ('Break-through' may be a more accurate description.) Or there may be no discernible crisis, just a general sense of futility and of being 'stuck' (very common in middle age!). We can go no further until we first go back and rediscover the bits of ourself that have got left behind. To recognise the need for this is itself the first step in renewal. The injunction 'Know thyself' is at least as old as the Delphic oracle of ancient Greece.

In 1975 Gerard Hughes, a Jesuit who had been chaplain to Glasgow University students, had reached such an identity crisis. After a fortnight alone on an island off the Scottish coast, he spent ten weeks walking across Europe to Rome—a journey that proved quite as much an inner pilgrimage as an outer. In 1986 he reflected on this experience.

> The real obstacle on our journey to God is not heat, thirst, blisters, road blocks, or other people, but the inner workings of our own minds, our inherited and unquestioned ways of perceiving ourselves and the reality around us. These are the most threatening and frightening obstacles, and the most difficult to overcome . . .
>
> This new discovery had come to me during the walk, but I had not understood its significance. . . . The people I met were mostly welcoming and kindly, but occasionally I would come to a village where the locals were abrupt and unhelpful. After a few weeks I came to realise that people were kind and welcoming when I was feeling full of life and my feet were not painful; when I was tired and my feet were hurting, then villagers were abrupt and unhelpful! At the time I had no idea that I was projecting my subjective state on to them and making condemnatory judgements, which seemed to me to be objective. It was only after I had written *In Search of a Way* that I began to see the connection between this habit of projection and my difficulty in trying to write a book. Unconsciously I was selecting, from the past, disparaging remarks about my ability to write, which I had assimilated into my own mind and way of perceiving, accepting them as axioms to be obeyed and not questioned,

> and projecting them on to my present task of writing. On the walk I had caught myself projecting my thoughts and feelings on to other people; later, when trying to write, I caught myself projecting other people's comments from the distant past on to me. I began to see that both habits of projection were destructive distortions of truth, which can create imagined enemies by projecting our ills onto others and blaming them, while also leaving us feeling helpless and hopeless by projecting on to ourselves the disparaging remarks of others. This is not a new discovery; it has been known for centuries, but it is when we begin to spot it operating in ourselves that the discovery becomes exciting and all-important to us.[8]

The Way of discipleship sooner or later involves some from of retracing our steps from the surface consciousness of conventional adult life (with its necessary masks and roles) back through our various layers to our ultimate Source. As the obstacles to life and love at each level are dealt with, we become freer to serve God and our neighbour.

The traditional divisions of prayer (vocal, mental, and contemplative or mystical) are commonly seen as successive stages, progressing upward from lower to higher. They are better thought of as co-existing layers, ranging from the verbally articulate surface of personal consciousness down to the inarticulate, sub-verbal depths where our groanings cannot be uttered, and where God himself may seem as impersonal as our own mother did at first.[9] We still know very little about these sub-rational depths, but they are being stirred again in our day by the Spirit moving upon the face of the waters, and not only in the charismatic/pentecostal movement. For example, after some years in which many turned to Eastern religions to satisfy a spiritual hunger which was manifestly not being met in our activist Western churches, there is today a tremendous resurgence of interest in Christian meditation and contemplative prayer, especially in the Benedictine and Ignatian traditions, and in practices (such as the Jesus-prayer and praying with icons) learnt from the Eastern Orthodox churches. William Johnston now sees emerging a new Christian mysticism which learns from Eastern traditions of prayer while remaining firmly rooted in Christ and the Gospel.[10]

Many today find traditional descriptions of the Way of prayer unrecognisable, quite apart from the pious jargon. One reason is that the older writers take for granted that anyone literate enough to read them at all will already be sufficiently mature as a person to undertake without undue anxiety a personal discipline involving a measure of separation from the natural community. They take for granted previous experience of 'belonging' in such a community. They also take for granted a certain verbal fluency and, above all, personal consciousness and responsibility—in short, individuality. (This is sometimes pejoratively called 'middle-class consciousness' and very often confused with its abuse, individual*ism*.)

With the advent of compulsory schooling even for those who don't want it, none of this can any longer be taken for granted. Very many who are formally well educated are too insecure as persons to dare to think for themselves (and so risk alienation from their peer group); they are dangerously vulnerable to manipulation, and want nothing more than a safe role to protect them from ever having to wonder who they are. For very many today, their point of entry into the Way is therefore different—or rather, there are some long approach roads to be travelled first. You cannot undertake personal discipleship until you are a person.

4
In the Beginning

One reason why the gospel so often falls on deaf ears is that the gospel of creation must precede the gospel of redemption. It's no good proclaiming the love of God to those who are not sure that there *is* an actor behind the roles they play—and are terrified to look.

We have to go back to the beginning, before creation by the Word, to the pre-verbal, pre-natal darkness on the face of the deep, to where the earth is without form and empty of meaning—because that is where a very great many people today are. (Most will do almost anything to avoid facing that terrible void: this is the deepest root of modern Western man's compulsive busyness, and of the addiction to background noise by day and sleeping pills by night which shields one from ever having to think). Here, in Genesis 1, is the existentialist abyss of non-being, the bottomless pit of those nightmares of falling in which ontological insecurity manifests itself. Here is the undifferentiated chaos of which creation is evoked by the Word and into which (so we are told both by ancient myth and by the Second Law of Thermodynamics) the ordered cosmos will one day return.

A good deal of it already has. The twentieth century has watched painting and sculpture renounce the visible world of appearances with its laws of proportion and perspective. Serious music abandons tonality and form, while in popular music the European soul yields to the tribal drum. The novel has loosened its grip on plot and character. We have had the 'theatre of the absurd' and the 'happening'. Philosophy no longer looks for meaning. Even theology, once the Queen of Sciences which gave meaning to all the others, has long since become just one among many specialised subjects studied within the framework of the 'modern' scientific world view. (In fact that world view's presuppositions are those of the eighteenth-century Enlightenment, rooted in Bacon's quest for 'value-free facts' unrelated to any end or purpose, in Newton's mechanical physics, the sceptical philosophical method of Descartes and the insistence of the English empiricists that anything that cannot be tested scientifically is rubbish.) Language itself disintegrates: the verbal currency is devalued by a mindless flood of words from the mass media; rational discourse is displaced by sub-verbal images. The solid structure of moral values has crumbled, and with it any authority capable of commanding respect. Western culture since 1918 has been torn between recognition and evasion of the death of Christendom. We can no longer take anything for granted.

Nor can the editors of Genesis. Their ordered cosmos has collapsed with the fall of Jerusalem. (Whether the 'end of the world' ever becomes a physical fact or not, it is a recurring psychic experience for those who keep on growing, each time new knowledge shatters old certainties.) In an alien land, the exiles find that they still exist—as Jews, distinct from their Babylonian neighbours. They learn that their identity no longer depends on their environment but on their God, now recognised for the first time in the full glory of his transcendence, yet also mysteriously very near to the lowly and penitent individual: 'Thus saith the high and lofty One that inhabiteth eternity, whose name is Holy: "I dwell in the high and holy place, with him also that is of a contrite and humble spirit"' (Isaiah 57.15). The Hebrew exiles choose to be faithful to the God who brought them out of Egypt, and he now quite literally saves them from non-being. Second Isaiah is full of this.

The vision of Second Isaiah is born of affliction. Like Jacob, the children of Israel wrestle through the darkness with the Living God and thereby learn their new name, their true identity (Genesis 32.24–28). In Revelation 2.17 it is promised that the disciple who perseveres to the end will be told his unique identity, known only to him and to

God, of which the white stone is an archetypal symbol. Meanwhile God may hide his face; he may keep silent; he may stay his hand and let your enemies triumph; clouds and darkness may be round about him. But so long as (like Job) you keep on wrestling with him, demanding to know the *meaning* of it all, you know he is not dead. Your community shattered, the earth may indeed seem without form and void: you are thrust back into primal chaos, before creation. Darkness may indeed be upon the face of the gulf that yawns before you, but at the bottom even of that, God. Underneath are the everlasting arms (Deuteronomy 33.27): *you know*, for you have been held by them. You have heard the voice that speaks the creative Word: 'God said ... and it was so.' And you have believed, that you might have life.

This is where we come in, every one of us: held in the arms, hearing the voice, seeking the face that will smile on us and, in that act of recognition, give us our being. Genesis 1 may or may not have value as an 'objective' account of how creation might have looked to a hypothetical outside observer; the Bible is not very interested in hypothetical outside observers. Whatever else Genesis 1 also is, it contains for the perceptive some luminous reminders of how creation is experienced *from within* by each one of us as we come to consciousness.

Most of us regard a small baby simply as the object of our own considerations, from the outside. But from birth, and even before,[1] he is already a centre of growing awareness: sensitive, vulnerable, full of confused but terrifyingly intense feelings. We have forgotten.

In all religions, creation is represented as the creation of light. 'The coming of consciousness (says Neumann), manifesting itself as light in contrast to the darkness of the unconscious, is the real "object" of creation mythology.' The beginning 'can be conceived in the life of mankind as the earliest dawn of human history, and in the life of the individual as the earliest dawn of childhood. ... The dawn state of the beginning projects itself mythologically in cosmic form, appearing as the beginning of the world, as the mythology of creation. Mythological accounts of the beginning must invariably begin with the outside world, for world and psyche are still one.' The psyche 'experiences its own becoming as a world-becoming, its own images as the starry heavens, and its own contents as the world-creating gods'.[2] And its own unconscious as the waters under the earth: the much-maligned three-decker universe represents not so much geography as psychic reality.

But the earliest dawn of perception is even earlier. As we retrace the racial journey toward humanity, for nine months we experience a mystical union with an undifferentiated One which is at once the self and the universe. The womb is the homeland of pantheism.

As we grow, our experience of floating in an all-embracing sea (the 'great deep') gradually changes to one of being enfolded and held within a warm, living, moving body. We hear sounds, such as the mother's voice and rhythmic heart-beat, but only the sense of touch is fully operative—the most primitive and deep-penetrating of all the senses, even for adults. Time and space are not yet. Reality is not yet polarised into subject and object, for there is as yet no perceiving ego separate from what is perceived. Darkness is upon the face of the deep.

Of that primal, undifferentiated perfection there are many symbols, mostly some form of circle or sphere; they express the self-contained, unmanifest Godhead, without beginning or end, in pre-worldly perfection, prior to any process. In this perfection all potential opposites are still united: the mythical 'world parents' are not yet separated from their embrace. It is the perfect beginning, with the opposites not yet polarised into thesis and antithesis, and the perfect end, with the opposites reunited in synthesis and the world again at peace.

Such a symbol is the circle drawn by God in Job 26.10, Proverbs 8.27 and Isaiah 40.22. Another is the *uroboros* or circular snake-biting-its-own-tail[3] which is the primal dragon of the beginning, known to ancient Egypt, Babylonia and Phoenicia. It appears in the Old Testament as dragon and as Leviathan[4] and in the Apocalypse as the Primal Being (now recognised in the Risen Christ) who says 'I AM the Alpha and the Omega, the beginning and the end'—the Lamb slain from the foundation of the world. The *uroboros* is a common alchemical symbol, and alchemy (once practised by scientists as respectable as Isaac Newton and Robert Boyle) was perceived by Jung to be, like astrology, a primitive form of depth psychology, projecting contents from the unconscious onto the elements as astrology projects them onto the stars. The *uroboros* appears today in the healing medicine of Navajo Indian sand paintings, in the art of West Africa, Mexico, and India—and in the drawings of English schoolchildren.

In the initial stage, when ego consciousness is still on the infantile level, the world is experienced as maternal and all-embracing—both by early man and by the infant reliving this phase of evolution. One is held and nourished by the Great Mother, all one's needs being supplied without conscious effort or responsibility. It is the earthly paradise, which may later be yearned after in times of distress but which can never again be realised in adult life.

> Only at a very much higher level will the 'good' Mother appear again. Then, when she no longer has to do with an embryonic ego, but with an adult personality matured by rich experience of the world, she reveals herself anew as Sophia, the 'gracious' Mother, or, pouring forth her riches in the creative fullness of true productivity, as the 'Mother of All Living'.[5]

In between, as we shall see, the negative side of maternal ambivalence emerges as the devouring Terrible Mother in all her manifestations, the 'dragon' that must be slain if one is to become an independent person.

We start life in total oneness with our environment, rooted and grounded in the womb like a vegetable, literally in touch with our world, merged in the undifferentiated One beloved of mystics. The deepest nostalgia of the human race is for this lost paradise where each one of us has actually experienced freedom from want and from fear. Great religions are rooted in that nostalgia. Politics is more influenced by it than most politicians would care to admit. Utopias transfer the mythical Golden Age from past to future; revolutionaries, to the immediate and attainable future.[6]

Some people from time to time feel again quite vividly this primal sense of 'oneness with the All'. Such flashbacks may happen in connection with religious or aesthetic experience, but may also occur spontaneously. They can be induced by drugs and by certain disciplines of mind and body. Hindu and Buddhist mystics deliberately cultivate mystical experience and base their philosophy upon it. Some heterodox Christian mystics have done the same, but the central tradition of Christian mysticism warns against either seeking such experiences for their own sake or taking them too seriously if they occur: experiences, like appearances, can be deceptive, and a *feeling* of overwhelming certainty is no guarantee whatever of truth.

It is hardly surprising that mystics should have to grope for words when trying to describe sub-verbal experiences. One can only hint, suggest, and use imagery which one hopes may evoke recognition in the reader. Precision in such matters is as impossible as when talking about God; indeed, the two are not infrequently confused, and the name 'God' given to a psychological experience. God can of course reveal himself through any kind of experience, but he is not to be identified with any.

The problem with any 'revelation' is how to distinguish the voice of God from that of our own unconscious. We need to 'test the spirits' (1 John 4.1) by what we know of God from other sources, especially from the whole experience of the people of God from the earliest times recorded in the Old Testament onward. The first Christians soon learnt by experience which sorts of belief are 'sound doctrine'[7] and lead to wholeness of life in Christ, and which sorts lead to limitation or distortion of life, to regression, mental illness and spiritual death. The Gnostic systems, based on uncritical acceptance of mystical 'revelations', resemble both Oriental speculations and the theosophies which under one name or another keep recurring in the West. The spontaneous tendencies of the human psyche do not vary much, however diverse their cultural manifestations.

Unconsciousness (or pre-consciousness) is in fact our natural state. It is the state of 'mass man', not yet differentiated out from his environment: sub-personal and pre-moral. Neumann describes thus the perception both of archaic man and of early childhood:

> Man and world have not yet been divided into pure and impure, good and bad; there is at most the difference between that which works, is pregnant with mana and loaded with taboo, and that which does not work. But what works is pre-eminent, beyond good and evil. . . . The consciousness of archaic man is no more discriminating than a child's. There are good magicians and bad magicians, but their range of action seems far more important than the goodness or badness of the act. . . . Seeming evil is accepted as readily as good, and there is, apparently, not even the beginning of what man subsequently claims to experience and recognise as a moral world order.[8]

It is at this sub-personal, pre-moral level that modern industrial/technological society operates, even—or perhaps especially—at its most sophisticated levels. J. R. Oppenheimer, one of the scientists involved in the development of the first atomic bomb, said afterward that 'it is my judgement in these things that when you see something that is technically sweet you go ahead and do it and you argue about what to do about it only after you have had your technical success. That is the way it was with the atomic bomb. I do not think anybody opposed making it; there were some debates about what to do with it after it was made.'[9] And this was before the rise of the computer: nowadays, increasing reliance on computers and on the sorts of data which can be programmed into them means that more and more decision-making is done without reference to human values.

'Mass man' is the apathetically unawakened *lumpenproletariat* at the bottom of every sophisticated society, whose immemorial role as cheap energy alone is absolutely secure—or was, until mechanisation and automation began robbing them of even that meagre livelihood. Inevitably exploited by those more conscious, Israel-in-Egypt nevertheless have, in their oppressors, a built-in scapegoat to blame for all their ills, and hence also a blissful irresponsibility to which very many (confronted with the harsh realities of life) later crave to return.[10]

The increasingly complex technological and bureaucratic society which we in the West have allowed to develop makes an ever-increasing proportion of the population genuinely unable to cope. This fact ought to be on the consciences of the capable in their enthusiasm for 'progress': privilege brings responsibility, and we *are* our brother's keeper.

For all of us there is a perennial temptation to prefer security to the risks of freedom, but we must leave our pre-conscious paradise if we are to become fully human. To yield to psychic inertia is spiritual death. It is the sin of *accidie* or spiritual sloth, the refusal of light and life that underlies so much of the violence of our age, as bottled-up energies that should be creatively used go sour within and the dark, alien aspects of human nature which we refuse to recognise in ourselves are projected into the outside world in the form of political and other demonologies.

The most worrying aspect of the modern mass media is the way in which they inhibit growth and actually encourage regression. 'Mass man' is frighteningly vulnerable to suggestion and conditioning, and there is a substratum of this in us all. In this sub-personal layer of personalities, the axioms of behaviourist psychology are valid. At this prenatal level we *are* just a bundle of reflexes, *re*-acting predictably, and incapable of resisting or of acting responsibly. It is here that the hidden persuaders operate, and those who manipulate them have a vested interest in keeping us uncritical, passive, and only half conscious.

5
Exodus

It is with the greatest reluctance that we enter into consciousness, individually or collectively. Our very first cry is a scream of protest. But we cannot stay in the primal paradise where our life begins. Life itself demands that we be violently uprooted and cast out into a cold, frightening world. It is the primal separation, and it is very painful. Our birth is our first experience of death.

When we speak of the pangs of childbirth we usually mean the mother's, but the child experiences them, too. As between feeling torn apart and feeling crushed to death, there's not much in it. The mother at least understands what is happening; she has memories of a past when she was not in pain and reasonable expectation of a future when she will have forgotten the sorrow for joy that a child is born into the world. For the child, time is not yet: the anguish, long or short, is eternal—and meaningless. We have forgotten. It is too terrifying to remember, though some are haunted by it in the form of claustrophobia or other seemingly irrational fears. Severe birth trauma may impair the child's capacity to relate to its mother and indeed to women generally.[1]

Birth brings our first awareness of change. Even before our eyes can focus properly, the primal differentiation has taken place: 'And God divided the light from the darkness' (Genesis 1.4). Henceforth we fear the darkness which was once our home (for we are not meant to go back) and turn, plant-like, toward the all-revealing light.

'Only in the light of consciousness can man know,' says Neumann. 'And this act of cognition, of conscious discrimination, sunders the world into opposites, for experience of the world is only possible through opposites.'[2] As an earlier Jewish writer puts it, 'opposite evil stands good, opposite death, life; so too, opposite the devout man stands the sinner. This is the way to view all the works of the Most High; they go in pairs, by opposites' (Ecclesiasticus 33.14–15 JB).

Separation from the ground of our being also brings anxiety and a longing for re-integration. Throughout life, this anxiety will both spur us to growth and tempt us to regression. Since our first experience of change is painful, it's not surprising that many shrink from change later in life, nor that the 'descent' from pre-natal paradise is so often felt to be a departure from perfection rather than an advance toward it. A powerful tradition in human thought, at least as old as Plato, contrasts the imperfect and changing world of becoming with the unchanging, ideal world of being.

India has always been pessimistic. Nature can be a cruel mother in a land where drought bakes the earth into brick for years at a time and where even the life-giving rain comes in monsoon torrents. The plight of India's poor has always been too intolerable to be accepted as real: in Hindu thought, the material world in all its diversity, suffering and change—and especially the personal consciousness that makes us aware of it—is *maya*, illusion.

Modern physics, too, acknowledges that all that we can know of the material world is relative to the perception of the observer. Illusion it may be, but modern science, having emerged in a civilisation shaped by Judaeo-Christian belief in a Creator God, regards what we can know of creation as worth exploring, for 'God saw everything that he had made, and behold, it was very good' (Genesis 1.31).

For the pious Hindu, being born is literally a fate worse than death. His goal is to earn escape from the cycle of rebirth into *nirvana*: there all pain and separation cease, all change and differentiation are done away, and we are reabsorbed into the timeless, boundless, impersonal One out of which we came. It is a return to the primal consciousness of the womb, before the creation of time and space.

Meanwhile in this life the most desirable thing is mystical experience of union with the One, to be achieved through ascetic discipline and elaborate techniques for entering into the self. Self is the only true reality.

Some of the techniques are of great value in themselves for mental and physical health, but the Christian's goal is different, for the Christian understanding of the self is different. We seek a personal relationship (not an impersonal merging) with an Other who *is 'other'* and who is already a society of Persons. 'They are to be one, perfectly one, as Jesus is one with the Father (says William Johnston, commenting on Jesus' prayer for his disciples in John 17.21). And yet they are not one, for the Father and the Son are different persons. I myself believe that this experience of unity in diversity and of diversity in unity is the core of the Christian mystical experience. And it can only be attained through love.'[3] Elsewhere he observes that the chief difference between the Buddhist and Christian understandings of self-realisation is that in the Hebrew–Christian tradition the self is essentially relational.[4] As John V. Taylor, then General Secretary of the Church Missionary Society, pointed out in his June 1969 *CMS-Newsletter*, 'the quest for absorption into Ultimate Reality and for the loss of individual identity means a profound denial of the otherness of the other, whether God or fellow man, and a rejection of distinctiveness and of choice. The pursuit of such a union is a flight from the demands of communion.' It is a regression to the pre-consciousness of infancy.

The relationship which Christians desire is neither achieved by any disciplines nor earned by any merit, but given: 'we love because He first loved us' (1 John 4.19). Our first experience of personal relationship at the natural level is also given, long before we are capable of doing anything to deserve it.

* * *

There are powerful echoes of our experience of birth from the waters of the womb, and of the coming of light out of darkness, in the Holy Saturday liturgy for the kindling of the New Fire. The baptismal font, in which new Christians are 'born again', is a womb-symbol. The Easter Vigil readings encompass the whole drama of creation and redemption but focus on the Exodus, the primal redemptive act of God which is central to Jewish consciousness to this day, and on that other Exodus (Luke 9.31) which Jesus accomplished at Jerusalem through his death and resurrection.

'Out of Egypt have I called my son': thus the eighth-century prophet Hosea describes God's bringing his people to birth as a nation five centuries earlier. The calling is done through Moses. One determined Hebrew mother has seen to it that *her* son was saved from death and given the education appropriate to leaders of man (Exodus 2). Moses has been brought up at court as a member of the royal family-privileged, cultured, leisured. One day he decides to visit his own people. There he sees a flagrant injustice done to a Hebrew by an Egyptian. He must often have seen such things done to slaves, but this time he suddenly realises that *he* is one of *Them*: brought up as a top-dog, he identifies himself with the underdogs. Impulsively he takes the law into his own hands—and then flees, both from retribution and from his privileged position. He finds his way to an oasis in the desert and attaches himself to the entourage of a wealthy sheikh, whose daughter he marries.

In a shepherd's life there is time to think. What Moses learns from his father-in-law echoes his own people's traditions, and he identifies Jethro's desert God with the God of the nomadic Abraham. At the mountain at the back of the desert Moses has his vision of God, *this* God, in the burning bush. This God is not territorial: if he was with Abraham in Haran and then in Canaan, and now with Moses in the Sinai, he must be in Egypt also. Moses receives his call to mission: to go back and tell his people about their desert God and to lead them out into the wilderness to worship him.

The good news for Israel-in-Egypt is that they have a

Living God who sees their predicament, who cares, and who has power to bring them out—if they will trust him. This they agree to do, though second thoughts arise when the cost of trusting him begins to be evident. Their nerve fails them at the Red Sea and it takes all Moses's genius as a leader of men to keep them from turning back:

> 'Fear not; stand firm, and see the salvation of the Lord, which he will work for you today. . . . The Lord will fight for you, and you have only to be still . . .'
> Thus the Lord saved Israel that day from the hand of the Egyptians. . . . And Israel saw the great work which the Lord did against the Egyptians, and the people feared the Lord; and they believed in the Lord and in his servant Moses. (Exodus 14.13–14, 30–31)

The significance of the Exodus can hardly have been apparent at the time to those experiencing it, any more than the significance of our own birth is apparent to us at the time. Only in retrospect does our birth become something to be celebrated annually as a means of affirming our unique identity. So it was with the Exodus.

It must in fact have been a fairly small group who shared this crucially formative experience, for nowhere in the Sinai is there enough water for more than a few hundred people (perhaps a thousand at most) to survive together for any length of time—to say nothing of the impossibility of keeping a horde of many thousands together in the winding wadis of that mountainous peninsula.[5] The numbers suggested by Exodus 12.7 must have been deliberately inflated by Torah-narrators of later centuries (who cannot have been ignorant of desert conditions) in order to stress the theological importance of the Exodus by comparison with events of their own time—a common device in oral tradition. In retrospect it had become clear that it is *here* that Jewish identity is rooted, rather than in the exploits of kings ('Saul has slain his thousands, and David his ten thousands'—1 Samuel 18.7).

Not all the Hebrews went down into Egypt. In particular, it seems probable that those settled in the Shechem area in the days of the patriarchs were still there when Joshua arrived. (There is neither record nor archaeological evidence of any conquest in that central area, which suggests that it was already in the hands of kinsfolk; and Genesis 33.18–20; 34; 35.4 and 37.12 link Jacob's clan with Shechem.) The incorporation into the Exodus faith of those who have not shared the Exodus experience is described in Joshua 24—an account probably written down in the time of Deuteronomy, six centuries after the event. At Shechem, the covenant made with the followers of Moses at Sinai is extended to include the whole assembly of Israelite tribes.

(The same thing happens again after the Exile, when the minority who return to Jerusalem under Nehemiah understand their return as a second Exodus and impose their faith and practice on those who have not experienced the Exile (Nehemiah 8–13). It is at that time that the Book of Joshua reaches its final form.)

The people continually lapse into the local cults. The temptation must be almost irresistible. As the Hebrews settle in Canaan, they learn from the Canaanites the agricultural way of life with its yearly cycle of festivals through which the Canaanite priests teach their people when to plough and plant and reap. In traditional village agriculture even today, religious rites are as integral a part of agricultural science as ploughing and planting, and to omit any detail is to court disaster. The first Hebrew farmer who dared *not* to sacrifice to Baal was a brave man; you get the feel of it in the story of Gideon's destruction of his father's altar to Baal in Judges 6.7–32.

The Hebrews are taught by their priests to link the all-important agricultural festivals, not with their Canaanite neighbours' fertility myths about gods and goddesses, but with the mighty acts of Yahweh in history, beginning with the Exodus. Pagan gods, thought to control various forces of nature, have to be persuaded, annually, to bestir themselves into action at the appropriate time. Yahweh, who against all the odds actually rescued a slave people from Egypt, himself takes the initiative, and in the covenant with Noah (Genesis 8.21–22, 9.8–17) has guaranteed that the agricultural cycle will never cease. You no longer have to persuade the gods each year to act; instead, you give thanks to Yahweh because he *has* acted and *does* act.

Because many of the local country shrines were originally dedicated to Baal, the Deuteronomic reform in the seventh century BC aims to centralise all sacrificial worship 'at the place the Lord your God shall choose', i.e. at Jerusalem. And it is with the ancestral experience of the Exodus, some six centuries earlier, that the Deuteronomist tells the worshipper of his own day to identify himself. As he brings his harvest festival offering, the Hebrew farmer is to say:

> A wandering Aramaean was my father; and he went down into Egypt and sojourned there, few in number; and there he became a nation. ... And the Egyptians treated *us* harshly, and afflicted us, and laid upon us hard bondage. Then *we* cried to the Lord the God of our fathers, and the Lord heard our voice, and saw our affliction, our toil, and our oppression; and the Lord brought *us* out of Egypt with a mighty hand and an outstretched arm, with great terror, with signs and wonders; and he brought us into this place and gave us this land, a land flowing with milk and honey. And behold, now I bring the first of the fruit of the ground, which *thou*, O Lord [not Baal] has given me.
> (Deuteronomy 26.5–10)

* * *

Who were the Hebrews?

'A wandering Aramaean was my father': a maverick, a 'nobody'. No proud ancestry here!

In the unstable world of the little warring city-states of the ancient Near East, whenever a new ruling group took over (pushing the old élite down the social scale) or whenever population growth led to overcrowding and shortage of water and food, those at the bottom of the heap would become outcasts. They would get some sheep and goats and wander in the hill country between the towns and villages—sometimes raiding, sometimes trading, sometimes hiring themselves out as mercenaries. They were not true Bedouin, for they were always looking for somewhere to settle again.

Such, apparently, were the semi-nomadic Habiru (or Hapiru) mentioned in the Tell el-Amarna letters, written by various Egyptian governors of Palestine and Syria to ask help in repelling these marauders, a century or two before the time of the Exodus. We cannot of course be certain of the identification of the Habiru (or some of them) with the Hebrews, but it seems likely. Some of them had already drifted into Canaan before Abraham, and some of these moved down into the Egyptian delta in a time of severe drought. Abraham is described as a wealthy sheikh who left home voluntarily in response to a call from God. But famine is no respecter of persons and his family, too, sought refuge in Egypt.

Those whom Moses leads out of Egypt include a 'mixed multitude' (Exodus 12.38). What gives the children of Israel their identity is not physical descent but the sharing of spiritual experience. It is so to this day. A significant proportion of Jews of the Dispersion are at least partly descended from converts.[6] But it is with the archetypal experience of the Exodus that all Jews identify themselves year by year in the Passover liturgy (Exodus 12.24–27; 13.3–16).

Jeremiah, writing just before the fall of Jerusalem to the Babylonians, foresees his people's eventual return as a second Exodus:

> The days are coming, says the Lord, when men shall no longer say 'As the Lord lives who brought up the people of Israel out of the land of Egypt', but 'As the Lord lives who brought up and led the descendants of the house of Israel out of the north country and out of all the countries where he had driven them. Then they shall dwell in their own land.' (Jeremiah 23.7–8)

In the Exile, Second Isaiah speaks of Israel's return to

Jerusalem in language reminiscent of the Exodus. When some of the exiles actually do return, however, it becomes only too clear that the looked-for Day of the Lord has not yet come—the day, proclaimed by prophets from Amos onward, when God will complete the work of redemption begun in the Exodus.

In our Lord's time many in Israel are looking for the fulfilment of the promises. Some, among whom are the Essenes, have come to believe that at the Last Day only a faithful remnant will be saved, who must meantime keep themselves separate. Then, as now, not all Jews are messianic: certainly not the worldly Sadducees, who have a vested interest in the status quo, and probably not the majority of the Jews of the Dispersion. But in Judaea and the Galilee, where Roman rule is most resented, messianic hopes run high, especially among the Zealots—though most are thinking in political terms, forgetting the prophets' call for repentance.

The prophetic call is sounded again by John the Baptist, and taken up by Jesus in his own preaching of the kingdom of God. Luke, in his account of the Transfiguration (9.31), sees Jesus's forthcoming death and resurrection as a second Exodus,[7] and the very first Christian preaching, by Peter on the day of Pentecost (Acts 2.14–36), proclaims that in the life, death and resurrection of Jesus the long-awaited Day of the Lord has finally dawned.

'Christ our Passover is sacrificed for us,' says St Paul (1 Cor. 5.7) and in our Easter hymns and liturgies we Christians identify ourselves with both the first Exodus and the second. Week by week in the Eucharist, the Christian Passover, we renew our participation in the New Covenant, now no longer for one nation only, but available for all.

It is in the Exodus that, for the first time in human history, the immemorial dance of life turns into a march. Here is the root of the secular human belief in progress; here begins that momentous shift in the focus of human longings, from a lost paradise in the past to a promised land in the future, which culminates in the vision of the heavenly Jerusalem.

6
The All-provider

After the primal transformation experience of birth, there follows a long formative process of psychic integration around an all-providing maternal figure. This need not of course be our natural mother. Anyone will do, *provided it remains the same person* and not a multiplicity of institutional staff or baby-minders. Especially during the first year of life, and if possible up to about three years, we need a *single*, stable mother-figure with whom to identify. It is through identification with her that we begin to discover our own identity. We are vulnerable to her moods and sensitive to her voice and smell and touch. We are totally dependent upon her recognition of us and her attention to us for our knowledge that we exist. This universal human experience underlies Berkeley's celebrated philosophical dictum *esse est percipi*, to be is to be perceived.

The mothering of a child through its first year of life is a staggering responsibility and privilege. It is as integral a part of the pro-creation entrusted to women by the Creator as the carrying of a child in the womb. In modern societies we don't always take this quite seriously, nor realise the consequences in later life of emotional deprivation at this crucial stage.

'Many-mothers' at this stage means an indeterminate psychic structure in the child. It is true that in traditional tribal societies children are collectively brought up at the later stages, but weaning is much later than with us (at two or even three years) and till then the infant spends much of its time slung on its mother's back or hip, in the closest possible contact.

'No-mother' (whether actually absent or emotionally remote) means psychic non-existence for the child if no other stable mother-figure (such as a grandmother, aunt, or older sister) is available. So does an emotionally intense or possessive mother, whose 'overpoweringness' inspires anxiety and terror rather than trust. Sometimes the father or an older brother provides an alternative masculine identification-figure and source of 'mothering' affection.[1] If no adequate substitute is available, you cannot even begin to become yourself. We ought to have more compassion than we usually do for those lonely infant souls in adult bodies behind whose compulsive craving for attention lies a desperate quest for assurance that they exist.

Identity-seeking self-assertion can also be a collective phenomenon, as when groups feel 'left out' force their existence upon the world's attention, often with infantile aggressiveness and a pre-moral, sub-personal disregard of the cost to others. Terrorist behaviour is at bottom infantile behaviour. So is amoral power politics ('might makes right'). So is any form of cruelty, whether insensitive or sadistic; so is the manipulation of people, whether for personal, political or commercial motives: *other people are not yet recognised as persons*, only as objects in the environment, as *things* to be exploited for one's own benefit, satisfaction or amusement.

Many things which in later life are sinfully inappropriate—avarice and its frustrated twin, envy; gluttony for limitless indulgence in food, drink, sex and other forms of sensual gratification; lust for power and for domination or possession of other persons—are rooted in the necessary 'devouringness' of the infant at the breast. We draw our nourishment then (if we are lucky) from our mother's flesh: the only reason why we are not cannibalistic is that we do not yet have any teeth.

For the infant, time is not yet: in the mother's presence is eternal life; in her absence, eternal non-being. We experience this again consciously later in life when we fall in love. The love of the infant for its mother, and the love of the lover for the beloved, is the dependent, needy love which the ancient Greeks called *eros*. This is something much more fundamental than mere sexual attraction, though of course it includes that. It is the instinctive upward-striving of all living things toward the Good, the True and the Beautiful, as a plant turns toward the sun. *Eros* is the energy of life which powers evolution and overcomes the downward drag of entropy. It is the natural energy underlying all our highest aspirations, including our response to God. (Of our yearning for God, the fourteenth-century English author of *The Cloud of Unknowing* observes that 'by love he may be gotten and holden; by thought, never'.[2])

Sexual cravings belong to the sub-rational infant layers of our personality, which is why they are so intense. It's hardly surprising that mystics so often use the imagery of sexual love, nor that there is a mystical element in sex: both belong to the same sub-verbal level of experience.

When two mature persons, secure enough in their own identities to meet without merging, respect and love and trust one another sufficiently to undertake the commitment of marriage, the glorious irrationalities of sex are safely contained within the context of wider relationships and responsibilities. This is the normal way in which most ordinary men and women reopen communication with the infant depths of their own personalities, completing and integrating one another at the deepest possible level. Sexual promiscuity, on the other hand, has a dis-integrating effect on the personality, as St Paul was well aware (1 Corinthians 6.15–19).

Polite Victorian society was shocked when Freud spoke of infantile sexuality. They'd have been even more shaken if they had been able to recognise that adult love-making is itself essentially infantile, involving as it does regression to that level of consciousness where absorption in the sense of touch is almost total—a regression that must include, at the appropriate moment, letting go one's hard-won rational control. The longing for merging with another is a longing to return to primal union.

The way of celibacy involves a different encounter with

one's own depths and with the contrasexual 'other' within: for a man, with his unconscious feminine *anima* (to use the Jungian term); for a woman, with her unconscious masculine *animus*.[3] Celibacy involves different disciplines and responsibilities, and different ways of learning to love without possessiveness. It has its own rewards, not least in a kind of spiritual parenthood rarely possible for those who have given hostages to fortune through marriage and family life:

> Sing, O barren, thou that didst not bear; break forth into singing, and cry aloud, thou that didst not travail with child: for more are the children of the desolate than the children of the married wife. (Isaiah 54.1 AV, quoted by St Paul in Galatians 4.27)

But as Johnston observes, celibate love is not only for celibates.

> Married people are also called to practice profound celibate love. When married persons devote themselves to the service of the poor and afflicted and the oppressed, they practice celibate love. When they love friends and relatives other than their marriage partner, they practice celibate love. When they love one another and refrain for a time from sexual relations—and, as we know, married people sometimes feel called to practice such continence—their love is celibate. And often they experience, no less than consecrated celibate people, the power of such celibate love. . . . Celibate love is an integral and powerful part of the Christian life, whether that life be lived in marriage or in virginity.[4]

'The goal of psycho-sexual maturity is not orgasm; it is the capacity to love,' says another recent writer.[5] 'Whether a person becomes a celibate or marries, the same maturity, by which I mean acceptance of oneself as a sexual being and the ability to live with impulses and integrate them into oneself, is something all of us will need to grow into as we strive to achieve full humanity.' What we all need, he says, is intimacy: an unfeared self-disclosure in which we let the masks drop and share our real identity. And it is through our friendships that all of us, celibate of not, fulfil our need for intimacy.

> Intimacy in human living is important for personal growth, self-esteem and for a feeling that life is worth while. The more we live in a mass society, the more important are intimate relationships to maintain our individuality and identity. The basic need, then, is intimacy, not genitality. If this need is satisfied, the need for genitality is lessened.

This is true whether one's orientation is heterosexual or homosexual.

Much of what we label sexual 'perversion' represents a fixation in infantile phases of relationship (whether of attraction or revulsion) with parents and especially with the mother-figure.[6] This is especially true of paedophilia, which is responsible for so much child abuse. The 'deviant' is a peculiarly vulnerable scapegoat, embodying (even when he does not act out his fantasies) just those hidden impulses which the respectable most fear to recognise in themselves.

Homosexuality is a perfectly normal phase of growing up which most of us pass through: at the stage when we need a same-sex model outside the family circle, the schoolgirl typically falls in love with the games mistress, the boy with the scoutmaster. But the pattern of coming to consciousness seems to be first differentiation, then encounter and integration, leading to a wholeness which embraces diversity. In the light of this, inability ever to outgrow the phase of absorption in one's own mirror image and to move on to encounter with the 'otherness' of the opposite sex must seem a form of arrested development.[7] There are gloriously creative ways of using this state of affairs, which can bring with it acute sensitivity and perception, sometimes including artistic gifts of a high order, and great capacity for pastoral understanding and compassion.

To practise celibacy against one's inclination is an exacting discipline for heterosexual and homosexual alike. Whether a stable 'practising' homosexual relationship can ever be morally acceptable is something on which Christians are deeply divided. Certainly promiscuity, whether hetero- or homosexual, can never be.

One must of course distinguish between the homosexual *condition* and homosexual *behaviour*, for sexual orientation is not always a simple either/or; rather, there is a spectrum along which we find ourselves, so that some are sexually ambivalent. We are not responsible for our orientation, whatever it is; we *are* responsible for what we do with it.

What is certain is that the capacity to love, and to grow in love, does not depend on one's orientation.

Erna Hoch, a Swiss psychiatrist, worked for many years in India, where the old social order with its caste and joint-family system was breaking down under the impact of Western influences. She describes the growth of consciousness in terms which can also be understood as the growth of love.[8] She came to realise how closely mental illness is associated with difficulties of emerging from our primal union into personal consciousness and responsibility, and she identifies three stages in our emergence from that initial oneness.

'One first step from empathic oneness to differentiation between a "private world" and a "common world" leads to a level at which this "common world" is perceived and understood as a kind of liberal mother, from whom one can take without having to ask or thank.' This corresponds to the needy, dependent love which the Greeks called *eros*. 'This stage often persists, even in people who regard themselves as quite grown up. Many forms of what one calls "psychopathy" and of addiction, criminality and psychosis, are characterised by autistic behaviour of this kind.' Indeed, in our dreams we all behave thus: 'we take features from our fellow beings, we use them to stage our own little internal drama, without taking account of the true being of these people, without asking them for permission or thanking them and without feeling any obligation toward them.' Moreover, 'many people act in almost the same way in their waking life: their fellow world is of use to them only as a convenient object for exploitation, as a mirror in which to reflect their own glory, as a scapegoat for their own shortcomings'.

Most of us behave this way occasionally; the temptation to do so is never very far away. *Most of the world's problems—political, economic, social—are rooted ultimately in the infantile self-centredness of individuals and groups.*

'At the next stage (continues Dr Hoch) there is a growing awareness of the existence of fellow human beings who are equally alive and who have the same needs and rights as oneself.' Many people, she says,

> can break through into this second stage only by first experiencing the living resistance which another person can offer to some aggressive act. This happens normally to a certain degree in the phase of spitefulness of the three- to four-year-old child and again during the rebellious phase of the age of puberty. Once this stage is reached, a person assumes the character of an individual, and can approach his fellow human beings as equal to himself; he lives in a kind of 'brother world' and he keeps up a fairly well-balanced exchange of taking and giving between his 'private world' and the 'common world'.

This corresponds to the 'brotherly love' which the ancient Greeks called *philia*.

> Even then, plenty of defences and filters will be built in, so as to guard himself both against exploitation and against letting his anti-social impulses leak out into the 'common world'. If defences of this kind become too rigid and permanent, they may impose themselves as neurotic symptoms.
>
> This is the stage of many of our western societies, with their stress on equality and fraternity and on following 'the golden rule'. It also seems to have been the spirit of the early Christian communities.

In the final stage, 'a human being would arrive at an openness which, without any defences, allows the stream of life and love to pass through him from eternal sources to his fellow human beings, without expecting anything in return'. This corresponds to the self-giving love which the New Testament calls *agapē*. It has been defined as willing the highest good of the other, at whatever cost, to oneself or to the other. *Eros* depends on the inherent attractiveness of its object; even *philia* has its limits; only *agapē* can love the unlovable. Dr Hoch's use of the conditional 'would arrive' suggests how rare is the actual achievement of this ideal in practice. 'At this stage alone, free from any ambitions and aspirations of his own, man can be entirely receptive to the needs and problems of his fellow human beings without bringing in his own distortions. In the light of the purified consciousness of a person of this kind, others will then be able to grow into what they are meant potentially to be, and not merely into poor distorted products of the pressure of an imperfect society.'

So the disciple's perseverance toward full personal maturity is no selfish quest, but contributes mightily to the well-being of others. God saves the many through the faithful few.

* * *

Our mother is the source of our being at the natural level. She is our first substitute for God, and our experience of her in infancy colours our experience of God in later life as well as our capacity for personal relationships. The anti-social adult has commonly had an unsatisfactory experience of mothering: either too little, or (in the absence of an adequate father-figure) too much. Our experience of that primal relationship also shapes our deepest metaphysical assumptions, e.g. as to whether the world around us is trustworthy or capricious, and whether life itself is a good to be embraced or a fate to be endured. Here, in our initial experience or acceptance or rejection, are laid the foundations of our future self-respect—or depressive self-hatred.

We are made into persons by being treated as such and not as a noisy, dirty, hungry, wriggling *thing* which must be bathed and fed and endured until it is able to carry on a rational conversation. God alone knows how much of the alienation of modern young people begins with 'emancipated' mothers who are bored with babies. Not every mother (or father!) is capable of meeting the emotional demands which an infant or toddler *must* make of someone. Many have unsolved infantile problems of their own, the intolerable pain and anxiety of which are evoked by an infant's crying or a toddler's rage. This is the root of the 'battered baby' syndrome, and of much parental rejection of 'difficult' older children and teen-agers.

Our experience of even the best of mothers is bound to be ambivalent because of our total dependence. But to the extent that anything goes seriously wrong in that primal relationship, *no other can ever be more than role-play*, unless or until that primal deprivation has been dealt with. We cannot skip stages.

People who lack social confidence or are 'shy of participating' are usually too unsure of their own identity to be open to others. It is cruel and useless to nag at them: to hold up what is for them an unattainable ideal can only confirm their sense of inadequacy. For those who have as yet no clear boundaries to their own personalities, *any* real encounter threatens invasion, possession, and risk of being devoured by (or else devouring) the other. For them, Sartre's dictum is true: 'Hell is other people.' Such folk need first to experience, if only briefly and perhaps in a clinical setting, the security of relating to some 'parental' source-person who accepts them as they are and with whom they can identify for a time, until their own ego has acquired sufficient substance to survive independently.[9] Until this has happened, they are too vulnerable to risk group-involvement. Even a 'healing community' may be experienced as a threat. (If such folk become involved in group dynamics—sometimes, incredibly, miscalled 'sensitivity training'—serious breakdowns can result. They are far too sensitive already.)

The seeing eye learns to recognise folk who are still hunting for their source-person in order to get started. They form no small part of a priest's or minister's pastoral burden, for the very fact of being ordained or set apart makes one an obvious carrier for other people's projections. Thus one shares in Christ's taking away of the sin of the world. ('Christ clothed himself in the archetypal images,' says Austin Farrer, 'and then began to do and to suffer.'[10]) It is a costly ministry. So was it for him on whom the Lord laid the iniquities of us all.

The technical term for the projection of parental images and relationships onto other persons is 'transference'. It is an important part of the normal learning process.[11] The mature are often called upon to play the parental role to others than their own children. Whole professions involve this: nursing, teaching, social work, and various forms of ministry and counselling. But we need to be alert to recognise the phenomenon of transference if we are to use it creatively and not ourselves be drawn unawares into the psychic collusion of counter-transference. We need to learn the warning signs of a person's needing professional therapeutic help: the pastor is often the first to whom symptoms of emotional disturbance (usually unrecognised as such) are presented, in the guise of moral or spiritual problems. (Sharp resistance to any suggestion of their true nature is itself one of the surest signs of their true nature! There is nothing the human race fears so much as self-knowledge.) The pastor needs wisdom, patience and tact, as well as maturity and insight.

Though to an external observer we are quite separate from our mother from the moment of birth, it takes us some time to grasp this momentous change. The distinction between 'Me' and 'Not-me' is first learnt through encounter with hard, unyielding objects: the physical boundaries of our personality are established by the simple expedient of kicking anything within reach. Proverbs 8.27 and Isaiah 40.22 speak of the circle which God draws upon the face of the deep: as we, too, learn to 'draw the circle', we define the area of experience within which we can create order and keep out the chaos beyond.[12] It is at this stage that we discover the sovereign power of thought, which is at the root of both magic and technology: the hand in front of my face, and the foot lower down, *do* what I *will* them to do! *I* can dominate nature; I can *act*! For the first time, we can make the tremendous affirmation of our own existence: '*I am*' (Exodus 3.14).[13]

The discovery of the physical boundaries of our personality is the first stage in the long, slow emergence of the dry land of consciousness out of the boundless sea of the unconscious (Genesis 1.1–10). The speed and final extent of this differentiation of personal consciousness varies greatly in different cultures and is much affected by child-rearing practices.

The world of infancy is the matriarchal world of the Great Mother goddess, benevolent or terrible as she gives or withholds her bounty. To this phase also belongs the Good Shepherd, who is a male 'mother', carrying the young lambs in his bosom (Isaiah 40.1). Moses is such an all-providing identity figure for the children of Israel in the wilderness.

The Exodus out of Egypt is *into* the social and cultural vacuum of the desert. It is a place of aridity and of boredom. Detachment from familiar landmarks and routines brings disorientation: no more making bricks without straw, but also no more brick walls and a roof over your head. Silence, solitude and freedom from distraction make possible interior vision and self-knowledge—and confrontation with enemies within. Beyond the circle of light from the camp-fire lies the 'howling wilderness' peopled by the demons which desert-dwellers project onto the blank screen of the emptiness around them.

It is in just such unstructured situations that charismatic manifestations of the Spirit are likely to erupt, which it is why it is among the rootless and the detribalised that Pentecostal Christianity spreads like wildfire. The African and other Independent churches with their charismatic founder-prophets (and prophetesses!) and their lack of formal structures belong here. So do the Hasidic Jewish communities with their 'rebbes'. So do all social groups (from tribe to religious sect to teen-age gang) in which authority is personal and charismatic rather than institutional

This is notably the case in the traditional culture of the Arab world to this day, and also in those of Sicily and southern Italy, the Balkans, Corsica, Spain, Latin America, and in most tribal cultures. Leadership is authenticated by conspicuous power and possessions, and in the absence of institutions which could transcend blood ties, the only way to change leaders is by a successful power challenge. Violence is expected—and respected; it is reconciliation which is shameful. The overwhelming importance of 'honour' prevents any appeal to rational principles such as human rights or the rule of law; equality is anathema, and compromise a sign of weakness.[14]

To this phase belongs the kind of primal kingship on which the well-being of the tribe depends, and also the 'benevolent despotism' of absolute monarchies and dictatorships, which are often well-meaning and even idealistic in theory, however oppressively they may be experienced in practice. Welfare states also partake of the nature of the All-Providing Mother.

Mount Sinai is the archetypal place of divine revelation. In Jewish tradition, it is here that God gave, through Moses, both the written Torah (i.e. the Pentateuch, the first five books of the Hebrew Bible) and also the 'oral law' (the Mishnah) which interprets it.

But revelation is not always welcomed. To the children of Israel in the Sinai, God appears in volcanic majesty and terror: in his holiness there is nothing of stained-glass piety or sanctuary slippers, but a pillar of fire and cloud erupting from the lower parts of the earth and thunder and lightning descending from heaven (from beyond the normal range of human perception) and echoing around the mountain-tops and wadis. Nothing less can penetrate the armour of apathy. So unwelcome is the disturbance that the people beg Moses, 'Speak thou with us and we will hear, but let not God speak to us, lest we die' (Exodus 20.19 AV).

But a sufficient measure of confrontation, mediated through Moses, is accepted and they enter into the Covenant relationship with the God who has saved them and who sustains them—the relationship which establishes their identity as the chosen people of God (Exodus (24.3, 7–8).

The gathered group, conscious only of itself around its Leader, is an essential stage of formation. It is of necessity an introverted stage, for in the desert there are no neighbours to whom to relate, nor any geographical boundaries. ('Guide me, O thou great Redeemer, Pilgrim through this barren land,' says the hymn.) So with the infant in its mother's arms: the rest of the world, as yet, hardly exists.

The Covenant is with a righteous God who demands righteousness. In ancient Middle Eastern paganism the point of sacrifice was to *make* the gods 'righteous'—to persuade them to pay attention and to act at the appropriate time. Thus Elijah taunts the prophets of Baal: 'Cry aloud, for he is a god; either he is musing, or he has gone aside, or he is on a journey, or perhaps he is asleep and must be awakened' (1 Kings 18.27). But in Hebrew religion, Yahweh *is* righteous, always; *he acts*, on his own initiative (not ours). His righteousness is his will and purpose (not ours): 'I will be what I will be' (Exodus 3.13–14). When we respond appropriately to his initiative and live according to his will and purpose for us, we are righteous.

At this stage, as in the nursery, morality is a matter of 'Thou shalt. ... Thou shalt not: I am the Lord.' It is through unquestioning obedience that we first learn what appropriate behaviour is. The time of personal responsibility is not yet.

The early stages of spiritual direction are sometimes experienced thus, as a kind of total dependence on a 'guru'. It is so for our Lord's little group of disciples as they live and walk about together—until his physical presence is taken away, and they suddenly have to grow up.

7
Conquest

The second separation-crisis starts with weaning and, as at our birth, our demonstrations of protest are anything but non-violent. We do not appreciate the compliment of being banished from our mother's arms and made to sit opposite her as a separate person to be fed. We become painfully aware that she is not our exclusive possession: there is father, perhaps brothers and sisters, and she has a life of her own which we cannot share. We learn the pangs of jealousy.

But if all goes well the psychic boundaries of our personality begin to be hammered out in the violent clash of wills between the frustrated infant ego and the parental firmness which holds infantile rage and aggression within safe limits. The conflict is disturbing to all concerned, but absolutely essential to the differentiation of consciousness. If at this crucial stage we do not encounter firm limits, we go through life looking for them, testing every authority, craving for someone who, by saying 'Thus far *and no further*,' will tell us who we are.

One cannot help wondering to what extent the adult craving for violence (e.g. in demonstrations deliberately aimed at provoking police retaliation, in football hooliganism, race riots, war, or 'dust-ups' outside the pub on a Saturday night) is a belated working-out of identity problems by those whose weary mums couldn't face the emotional cost of standing up to toddler violence. It is an undoubted fact that fighting does sharpen consciousness. So does competition of any kind. Contained within safe limits, human aggression and competitive striving are not only creative but absolutely essential to human growth.[1] The limits are also essential, whether they be the rules of the game or the rule of law. Moreover, though competition is an exhilarating stimulus in childhood and adolescence—and a permanently necessary spur to effort in a sinful world—it belongs to our immaturity and will not do as a social ideal for responsible adults.[2]

It is important to remember that we cannot be weaned until we have first been fed: we cannot skip stages. You cannot be separated out as a person if you have not yet become emotionally related. Those who have never known acceptance by an adequate mother-figure are too unsure of their identity to risk conflict: in the absence of parental affection and assurance, the need for at least minimal approval becomes desperately urgent.

Some adults are still looking for a parental figure, not to rebel against (toddler-fashion) but to cling to—seeking, with a bottomless hunger, for the total acceptance and affirmation and affection which an infant needs from its mother. The intensity and devouringness of the hunger are infantile, but because one is now physiologically adult, it is experienced as sexual attraction: one falls obsessively in love, typically with someone with whom actual marriage would be inappropriate or impossible. Many a disastrous marriage (or other liaison, hereto- or homosexual) does result, in which one or both partners make impossible emotional demands, for no one but God himself can satisfy another adult's ontological hunger. 'Thou hast made us for thyself,' says St Augustine, 'and our hearts are restless until they find their rest in thee.' Our mother (or mother-figure) is but the first of a lifelong succession of substitutes for God. Many of our problems in personal relationships are due to expecting from a friend what only Christ can give.

'I feel so easily rejected,' writes Henri Nouwen[3] concerning his relationship with his friend Jonas.

> When a friend does not come, a letter is not written, or an invitation not extended, I begin to feel unwanted and disliked. I gravitate toward dark feelings of low self-esteem and become depressed. Once depressed, I tend to interpret

even innocent gestures as proofs of my self-chosen darkness, from which it is harder and harder to return. Looking carefully at this vicious cycle of self-rejection and speaking about it directly with Jonas is a good way to start moving in the opposite direction.

Two things happened when Jonas and I spoke. First, he forced me to move out of the centre! He too has a life, he too has his struggles, he too has unfulfilled needs and imperfections. As I tried to understand his life, I felt a deep compassion and a desire to comfort and console him. I no longer felt so strongly the need to judge him for not paying enough attention to me. It is so easy to convince yourself that you are the one who needs all the attention. But once you can see the other concretely in his or her life situation, you can step back a bit from yourself and understand that, in a true friendship, two people make a dance.

Second, I learned afresh that friendship requires a constant willingness to forgive each other for not being Christ and a willingness to ask Christ himself to be the true centre. When Christ does not mediate a relationship, that relationship easily becomes demanding, manipulating, oppressive, an arena for many forms of rejection. An unmediated friendship cannot last long; you simply expect too much of the other and cannot offer the other the space he or she needs to grow. Friendship requires closeness, affection, support, and mutual encouragement, but also distance, space to grow, freedom to be different, and solitude. To nurture both aspects of a relationship, we must experience a deeper and more lasting affirmation than any human relationship can offer.

When all goes well, and the toddler who has already known adequate mothering experiences the security of loving restraint, the conscious ego becomes sufficiently separate from the mother to survive both the dereliction of her absence and also its own terrifyingly destructive hostility against her.

The creative miracle of speech now begins. Through the power of the word we begin to order the chaos around us and to share in creation out of No-Thing: 'whatsoever

Adam called every living creature, that was the name thereof' (Genesis 2.19 AV). We begin to find meaning and purpose in our environment, and meaning and purpose are as essential to man as food: without them, even with food in abundance, one loses the will to live; with them, one can survive almost any deprivation.[4] At this stage stories (fairy stories, myths, legends) are essential if the child's mind is to be stocked with the imagery needed in order to interpret and cope meaningfully with the experiences and relationships of later life. (And what better than Bible stories?)

With the coming of speech, time begins. We begin to understand the mother's absence and to trust in her future return: a separate identity is being formed, capable of surviving her absence. Memory and foresight enable us to transcend the present moment and to learn from experience. We embark upon the life-long discipline of learning to tolerate frustration and to wait.

The children of Israel learn this in the desert. Like an all-providing mother, God is there experienced both as beneficent and as terrible. The sign of his presence is the pillar of cloud by day and of fire by night: when it moves, they strike camp and follow; when it stays put—no matter for how long—they stay put (Numbers 9.15–23). Thus they learn to wait upon God.

Learning to tolerate frustration is central to growing up from the immediacy and spontaneity of infancy to spiritual maturity. It is no kindness to shield people from frustration or to get between them and their suffering. And patience, for most of us, is the most ordinary form of suffering (the very word comes from the Latin *patior*, to suffer). It is the beginning of the Way, and blessed are they whose mothers were willing and able to set their feet upon it.

Verbal fluency is crucial for the development of personality. Every perceptive teacher and parent knows the frustration of children who cannot express themselves in words, or whose vocabulary is very limited. In adult life, too, the need for self-expression through physical violence usually goes with inability to articulate one's thoughts and feelings in any other way. This is another aspect of the creative power of the Word to order chaos and give peace to men on earth.

It is at this stage that the real importance of fatherhood emerges. From the very start, the presence of a strong husband and father as the focus of authority in the household and primary object of his wife's affections protects the vulnerable infant from being swamped by its gigantic mother's emotional power. (There *are* giants in the earth in those days: see Genesis 6.4 AV.) But the primary function of fatherhood begins as speech establishes verbal communication and the beginnings of rational thought. 'In the beginning was the Word': the Hebrew revelation of God begins with rational consciousness, superseding the Great Mother religion of the unconscious pagan layers of our personality. This is why the rejection of paganism is so crucial for the people of God in both the Old and New Testaments—and in our own discipleship. (Abraham's original name, Abram, means 'the *father* is exalted'.) It is significant that in Hebrew the word for 'matter', *dabar*, also means 'word'. In Indo-European languages 'matter' is commonly from the same root as 'mother'—e.g. in English both words come from the Latin *mater*. (In Hebrew, 'mother' is from a different root.[5])

The father's proper task is to lead the growing child out from hearth and home into the wider world of adult responsibilities and relationships. What is usually called 'paternalism' (but more accurately '*ma*ternalism') is the maternal nurture which is essential to the infant but which (whether exercised by the mother or by the father) becomes to the growing child and adolescent increasingly suffocating. A child needs a strong father's help to cut the apron strings and escape from the seductive maternal indulgence and guidance which, if not checked, will continue its debilitating care and protection from cradle to grave.

True fatherhood is obscured, and our image of God thereby distorted, by human fathers who prostitute their masculine power to the reinforcing of an already-dominating mother's wishes ('You do as your mother says') or whose masculinity is so insecure that they must compensate for their inner weakness by blindly 'throwing their weight around'. De facto abdication of paternal authority is a constant temptation, whenever the men lose their nerve: behind the tribal elders wait the clan mothers; behind the king, the queen mother. In marginal circumstances it is usually the mother who holds the family together at subsistence level; in single-parent families the one who must play both roles is most often the mother.

There is an ancient ascetical tradition of 'flight from woman' which assumes (like the veiling of women in Islam) that grown men are incapable of self-discipline and must (like little boys) be shielded from temptation. 'Little boys' men often are, and of course women may be flirtatious 'little girls'. Men *are* more easily sexually aroused than women, but why should this cause *fear*? To locate the root of male fear in Eve's sexual seductiveness was, and is, an evasion of something too terrifying for the insecure to contemplate.

This explains the pathological resistance to knowing the deepest reason against the priestly ordination of women, and the emotional intensity of the debate about it. To attempt to 'be rational' about this deeply divisive subject effectively prevents the real issue from being faced, for it limits discussion to the surface level of human personality where conscious reasoning takes place (the visible tip of the iceberg) whereas the symbolic, sacramental priestly role as Catholic and Orthodox Christendom have always understood it operates primarily in the sub-rational nine-tenths. Most people are simply not yet conscious at that level—*and don't want to be*, so anything concerning that level is dismissed—often impatiently, sometimes angrily—as unreal or irrelevant in the face of what are perceived as overwhelming practical and political priorities. (The theological case can be argued either way, depending on the relative importance assigned to Christian tradition on the one hand and to the spirit of the present age on the other.) That the sacramental ministry has become politicised is part of the increasing secularisation of the Church.

Genesis accurately identifies the problem: Eve is 'the mother of all living', in her disturbing ambiguity. Not for nothing is the cult of the Great Mother the most archaic and pervasive form of religion. (St Paul tangled with her as 'Diana of the Ephesians'—Acts 19.28–34.) The very source of our natural life and object of our most elemental cravings is *also* (O fateful knowledge of good and evil!) at the root of our irrational anxieties and nameless terrors. To propitiate her anger and earn her favour remains, in countless disguises, the deepest religious impulse of all. 'Because thou didst hearken to the voice of thy wife' (Genesis 3.17): what Adam is rebuked for is being a hen-pecked husband. Eve's maternalism is the most fundamental of all the awkward facts of universal human experience with which God's scheme of redemption has to deal.

Matriarchy (in practice, though very seldom in theory) is the norm in pre-civilised agricultural societies. It is the women who conduct the hoe agriculture that produces the staple crop and who organise the economic life of the community, while their men hunt, fight, and engage in palaver (Proverbs 31.10–31). In a traditional rural Africa, a man taking a wife pays a bride-price to compensate her family for the loss of her labour; he clears a patch of ground, builds her a hut, and then expects *her* to feed *him*. It is estimated that 80% of Africa's food is grown by women, and the same must be true throughout much of the third world.

Civilisation depends in no small measure on escape from the mother as the *men* assume responsibility and initiative and seek new modes of cultural creativity to compensate them (with the loss of their 'hunter' role) for their lack of the natural fecundity of women. (The growing girl slips easily into her mother's role; the problem of civilisation is always the male role.) It is the men who conduct the plough agriculture whose increased productivity makes possible both a margin of safety against famine and also specialisation of functions and the richly differentiated society of town and city.

That Jesus reveals to us God as *Father* is thus no cultural accident. Whatever our conscious attitude, in the sub-rational depths of our personality men-in-authority are inescapably experienced as 'fathers'; women-in-authority, as 'mothers'. But *they are not interchangeable, for they operate at different levels of consciousness*. This is the crucial point. Father-figures belong to childhood, where they speak the word with authority and (in the normal, creative power-struggle between the generations) evoke conscious, identity-forming opposition. Mother-figures reign in the numinous *pre*-verbal layers of personality laid down in infancy, where their continuing domination prevents a separate identity from ever emerging. Hence for adults a mother-figure (whether experienced as benevolent or as terrible) is more regressive than a father-figure, for the regression is back beyond childhood to infancy. This is why so many find it disturbing to work under a woman executive: however wise and tactful, she cannot help activating in her subordinates buried infantile reactions. To be under a woman-in-authority is once again to experience part of oneself as a dependent tiny child.

For all men (and insofar as we become conscious we are all symbolically masculine[6]) the greatest perils-of-soul are those involved in the escape from the Great Mother. To be conscious at all is to resist her unconscious domination. The All-Providing Mother thereupon turns into the devouring Terrible Mother who fights to prevent the emancipation of her son/lover. Have we not all watched it happen? In discussing the difference between the religion of Baal of the Canaanites and of Diana of the Ephesians on the one hand and that of Yahweh on the other, J. E. Fison remarked in 1958[7] on the 'evidence all around us of the devastating effect of possessive parents (usually mothers) upon their children. The mother perhaps quite unconsciously exercises such a controlling grip upon her child that the boy or girl, tied to mother's apron strings, never really grows up to have a mind and will and character of his or her own.' He adds that 'such mother-possession is far too common in our modern Western world with its small families, and its attempt to prevent the break-up of the home is a most potent cause of that break-up'—something even more true today than when he wrote. Fison sees the relationship between Baal and his worshippers as one of mother-possession (Baal was the consort of the fertility goddess Ashtoreth), whereas Yahweh's religion begins with an exodus, a coming out of the womb of mother-possession.

To survive and become a person, the 'son' must turn the tables on the Terrible Mother, adopt her destructiveness and direct it against her. This is represented mythologically as the slaying and dismemberment of the dragon.[8]

> Awake, awake, put on strength, O arm of the Lord; awake, as in the days of old, the generations of long ago. Was it not thou that didst cut Rahab in pieces, that didst pierce the dragon? (Isaiah 51.9-10; cf. Exodus 3.14: 'I AM'). Was it not thou that didst dry up the sea, the waters of the great deep?

—not merely the 'reed sea' of the historic Exodus, but the bottomless abyss of the unconscious. In Revelation 21.1 there is 'no more sea', for when all is revealed, nothing remains unconscious.

It is to this dragon-slaying phase, when the establishment of a separate, conscious identity is paramount, that the liberation theology of Latin America belongs. In the Latin cultures of the Great Mother-dominated Mediterranean, the men have a deep need to be 'macho'. It is significant that the Christ brought to Latin America by Spanish Catholic missionaries was portrayed either as an infant in his mother's arms (the Madonna) or as a corpse in his mother's lap (the Pieta): a Christ who was born and died but never really lived.[9] In such a culture, the Christ of liberation theology is liberating indeed!

To this same phase belong the struggles for self-determination and autonomy of groups that feel oppressed by or excluded from a dominant culture, the violent revolutions and wars of independence through which colonies or oppressed minorities break away from mother countries, and the wars of conquest by which colonists and settlers occupy new lands.

The idealised account of the military conquest of Canaan in the Book of Joshua belongs here. We now know from archaeological evidence, as well as from the Book of Judges, that the reality wasn't quite like that. There was, for example, no walled city at Jericho from some centuries before Joshua until the city was rebuilt by Hiel the Bethelite in the reign of Ahab (1 Kings 16.24), more than three centuries after Joshua. The walls that 'came tumbling down', discovered by Garstang in the 1930s and attributed by him to Joshua's time, were shown by Kathleen Kenyon in the 1950s to be a thousand years earlier. In Joshua's time, there can have been little more than a squatter settlement there.[10] Hiel's contemporaries doubtless speculated as to how Jericho had come to be destroyed, but the Deuteronomic compilers were as far removed from Joshua's time as we are from the Hundred Years' War or the Black Death; the final (post-exilic) editors, still further. The whole archetypal saga represents what theologically motivated narrators thought *ought* to have happened: by the time of Deuteronomy and the Book of Joshua, the Exodus experience of a helpless band of refugees miraculously rescued from their oppressors had evolved into the 'top-dog' theology of the Chosen People. The whole saga has inspired many a people seeking a Promised Land, usually—as in the Puritan settlement of New England, the Afrikaner Great Trek in South Africa and the modern Zionist conquest of Palestine—at the expense of the people of the land.

'Dragon-slaying' is an essential phase of coming to consciousness, which accounts for the perennial popularity of St George. 'In the normal life of the individual (observes Neumann) the symbolic murder of the parents or its equivalent is a phase of development which cannot be omitted with impunity; often enough, as a large number of cases of retarded development have taught us, the advantage of being a "good child", who shrinks from the "murder" of his parents, is purchased at the perilous cost of the sacrifice of one's independence in later life.'[11] The 'crime' is felt as guilt, and it *is* ambivalent. But it is the essential act which sets man free: only then is 'he' born as a personality with a stable, separate ego. This is true for all, man or woman.

The young *man* must, in addition, become secure enough in his masculine identity to encounter Woman, no longer as the over-powering mother-figure, but as his equal—his young and beautiful bride. 'Why men seem to need more reassurance in their sexual role than women is related to three main factors,' observes Anthony Storr.

> First, in the sexual act itself it is necessary for the man to achieve and maintain erection, whereas the woman can remain relatively passive. Second, in the process of development from child to adult, the male has to take an extra step of emancipation; for he has to become a creature quite different from the mother, whereas the girl can remain more closely identified with her. Third . . . there is no male equivalent to child-bearing . . . Most societies have provided for the male's need for achievement by closing certain occupations to women and by emphasising the importance of the activities which then become the prerogative of the male.[12]

In tribal societies, initiation rites at puberty are intended to sever the boy from his mother and admit him to the society of men. The 'male-group' in all its manifestations is essential to the establishment of masculine identity in adolescence, and many men continue to need this kind of reassurance all their lives. The feminists know not what they do: equality of the sexes is no mean achievement, and to achieve it the men need a very long handicap! The wise will not begrudge it to them.

The human race is made in the image of God, and in our

flesh and blood the image is split into two. But maleness and femaleness in biological life are analogues of something far more fundamental. This emerges in C. S. Lewis's novel *The Hideous Strength* in a conversation between the Director and Jane Studdock, who (as a good feminist) has been resisting any notion of submission to the masculine:

> Yes, said the Director, there is no escape. If it were a virginal rejection of the male, He would allow it. Such souls can by-pass the male and go on to meet something far more masculine, higher up, to which they must make a yet deeper surrender. But your trouble has been what old poets called *Daungier*. We call it Pride. You are offended by the masculine itself: the loud, irruptive, possessive thing—the golden lion, the bearded bull—which breaks through hedges and scatters the little kingdom of your primness ... The male you could have escaped, for it exists only on the biological level. But the masculine none of us can escape. What is above and beyond all things is so masculine that we are all feminine to it.[13]

Which is why we rightly refer to God as 'He', and why the Word became flesh as a man and not as a woman.

All human personality, including our Lord's, is a mixture of masculinity and femininity. Jesus once likened himself to a mother hen (Matthew 23.57) and both Isaiah (66.13) and Hosea (11.3) speak of Yahweh as 'mothering' his people. Much that priests do, they do with the feminine side of their nature, and male 'mothers' can carry young lambs in the bosom and bring healing and peace to troubled souls without activating the Terrible Mother archetype which is so destructively potent in disturbed personalities. This is not to deny the negative associations which many have with father-figures. The point is that the Tyrannical Father archetype, however damaging, operates at a more-conscious, more rationally accessible, level where the damage can be more readily faced and dealt with.

In the Old Testament Yahweh is the husband of his people (Jeremiah 31.32; Hosea 2.16–20; Isaiah 54.5); in the New Testament the Church is the Bride of Christ (2 Cor.

11.2; Ephes. 5.23–32; Rev. 19.7–9; 21.2, 9). Orthodox and Catholic tradition sees the priest as an icon of Christ and, especially when celebrating the Eucharist, of Christ the Bridegroom preparing his Bride for the marriage supper of the Lamb. The Protestant understanding of ordained ministry, on the other hand, plays down the (sub-rational) symbolic aspects and stresses the (rational) ministry of the Word. There is thus less reason why women should not be Protestant ministers, though the mother-figure factor is operative even there.

There has in fact been in recent years a steady 'Congregationalising' of the church with a corresponding diminishing of the importance of the set-apart ministry and an enhancement of that of the ministry of the laity. The drop in the number of ordinands over the past thirty years is due in no small measure to the fact that a set-apart priesthood really belongs to stable, structured communities with clearly defined roles—to a Christendom that no longer exists. Nowadays much that was once done only by the ordained—preaching, pastoral work, theological teaching, retreat conducting, spiritual direction—is quite rightly done also by qualified lay people, women as well as men. It is ironic that women should clamour for ordination in the Age of the Laity.

The distinctively feminine contribution in the adult world is the communication of wisdom. The model is the 'wise woman' (her archetype is Sophia, the personified Wisdom of the ancient world) whom people can choose to consult (or not), who may prophesy, who holds up her hands in prayer while her menfolk hunt and fight, but who does not thrust herself upon you by being in a position of institutional authority. The seeress and prophetess were rightly respected in ancient Israel; the priestess was not, and this particular Hebrew taboo was a wise one. So is the immemorial Christian tradition.[14]

Whether we like it or not, womanhood belongs archetypally to the unconscious 'dark' side of creation. A woman's discipleship involves coming to terms, sooner or later, with this inescapable fact. Kick as we may against the pricks, if we persevere, we are brought at last to the Damascus Road. It is as if, after years of identifying as a matter of course with St George (as one must, to come to consciousness at all) you suddenly recognise that *you* are the *dragon*.

We daughters of Eve don't know our own strength, nor the depth of masculine insecurity. From time immemorial women have suffered much at the hands of men, who are of course physically stronger. No small part of this is undoubtedly a form of unconscious revenge, for no human being comes so close to wielding absolute power over another as the one who mothers an infant through its first year or two of life. As long as the human race continues to be born of women, so long will we women start *psychologically* from a position of strength. If we are to exercise our proper ministry in the Body of Christ we must learn to hold our hand. So must every mother do toward the babe in her arms, whose first image of God she is. So God himself in the Incarnation held his hand toward us, submitting to the limitations of the human condition. The celebrated 'under-achievement' of woman may represent a true instinct of women who are content to be women and not female men. The Tempter taunted our Lord with 'under-achievement'.

The real problem about women in the priesthood is that a priestess (by whatever name) is a living icon of the Great Mother goddess of infancy—our own and that of the human race—not of the God of Abraham, Isaac and Jacob, the God and Father of our Lord Jesus Christ, whose disciples we are called to be. And it is fatherhood, rightly understood, which helps us all, women and men alike, to grow up—more conscious, more mature, more responsible—toward the full-grown Man of whom Ephesians 4 speaks, to the stature of the fullness of Christ.

8
The Promised Land

The next integration is with the natural community. At this point we must pause to define some terms, for much muddled thinking results from indiscriminate use of the word 'community' to describe different types of group. William Temple used to distinguish three kinds:

(1) A *community* properly so called, he said, is a natural group based on kinship, locality, and ethnic or cultural affinity, e.g. tribe, clan, caste, traditional village or close-knit neighbourhood. Such a community embraces the whole of life. You share a group identity: 'I belong; therefore I am.' You can only belong, in this sense, to one community at a time. You have a role to play and custom and tradition to tell you how to play it. You can live comfortably all your life in such a community and never need to become an authentic person in your own right. Until modern times, most people did just that.

Even today the closed community, within which one belongs and outside which real people hardly exist, is a vital phase in our formation as persons. Boarding schools are temporary and powerfully formative communities; so are those day schools which have a distinctive identity and tradition. On the other hand, 'a school to which no one can belong save in a meagre sense of the word can never be a really potent educational medium,' says W. R. Niblett in *Education and the Modern Mind*. He describes John Middleton Murry's experience of passing from a London board school as a boy of eleven to Christ's Hospital: 'school ceased to be an external affair for him; he suddenly found himself endowed with ancestors and part of a community'.[1] Regiments and religious orders are communities which one can choose to join, and the wearing of a uniform or religious habit powerfully reinforces the sense of belonging. It is easy to condemn the 'old boy net', but for many in our rootless modern world their old school or regiment is the only community they have ever known; it has endowed them with ancestors and given them their identity. The 'class' thing, too, is really the community thing: a perfectly natural preference for one's own kind, who 'speak the same language'. Nationalism is simply tribalism writ large.

(2) An *association* is a voluntary group (club, society) formed to pursue some limited purpose or special interest, such as a hobby or sport, not necessarily shared by neighbours or kin. You can belong to any number of associations at once for different purposes. In practice, certain types of associations (trade union, political party, religious sect) may function as a person's community, drawing him into a group identity and dictating his social attitudes and cultural preferences.

(3) *Fellowship* (what the New Testament calls *koinonia*) links individuals who have each made a personal commitment to the same ultimate loyalty. They are *not* merged in a group identity, but each has, and keeps, his or her individuality. Fellowship embraces diversity, linking persons who may be from many different communities and cultures and who may have no natural affinity whatsoever.

The Church as we see it in the New Testament is the fellowship of the Spirit. It transcends all communities, including the Jewish community within which it was born. It is not itself a natural community, though it commonly exists within a community and may sometimes (as in medieval Europe) be virtually coterminous with it.

Those brought up within the Church's fellowship are likely to experience it at first as their natural community. And one of the things that happens to us in baptism is that we are adopted into that great kinship network which includes the glorious company of the apostles, the goodly fellowship of the prophets, the noble army of martyrs and the holy Church throughout all the world—and the angels and archangels and all the company of heaven. We become part of the people of God: we are endowed with their ancestors and entrusted with their tradition. Those who become Christians by their own choice as adults may be able to perceive the Church as a *koinonia* from the outset, but nowadays many need, for a time, to experience 'belonging' in a community.

It is fatally easy for the Church in particular times and places to regress into seeing itself simply as a natural community and to expect or even compel people to conform. This was the case with medieval Christendom, whose identity was hammered out in the long struggle against the encircling threat of Islam. (Muslim rule in Spain lasted from 711 to 1492 and the Turks besieged Vienna as recently as 1683.) The Latin church at the Reformation tried to impose itself as *the* community of a rapidly diversifying Western Europe and burnt its nonconformists at the stake, while Protestant counter-communities did the same, both with a zeal worthy of Saul of Tarsus. The ancient Syrian church in India, on the other hand, was content to be just one community among many others within India's immemorial caste system, and India was not disturbed—nor evangelised. In modern times, especially in the West, many people use their church as their club for religious activities—for many a nominal Christian is in fact a practising polytheist whose real gods may include status, affluence, power, respectability, and comfort.

* * *

The primary community is of course the family, which in many parts of the world still means a whole clan or kinship group. In the West today the family usually means only parents (or even a single parent) and children; the growing child may or may not experience a wider sense of community in neighbourhood, school, church, or nation. *Some kind of experience of belonging in a community is vital to growing up: without it, we remain rootless drifters.*

In tribal societies, puberty is marked by ceremonial initiation into full membership of the community. The initiate undergoes a painful ordeal (often including circumcision), symbolic of death to the child-role and rebirth into the adult-role. One is instructed in the communal traditions by which one will henceforth be guided. The ego is not yet autonomous, but functions as part of the group, and one becomes disoriented and 'lost' if excluded. (Excommunication is truly terrifying at this stage; tribal Africans have been known to pine away and die for no other reason than that they have been cast out and have lost the will to live.)

One is not yet altogether free of the Great Mother, for her maternal role has been transferred to the community, but she no longer reigns supreme and unchallengeable. We are now in the patriarchal world of gods and dragon-slaying heroes. Polytheism is natural to this stage. If, like the ancient Hebrews under the Covenant, you agree to worship only Yahweh, you are nevertheless aware that there *are* other gods. Where, as in medieval Europe, whole tribes become Christian, many a local deity survives as a 'saint'.

Traditional communities are stable, structured societies in which everyone has, and knows, his or her place. Recognised roles tell you who you are: king, priest, prophet, warrior, craftsman, peasant, husband, wife. Marriages are arranged between families with minimal regard for personal preference. There are rules to tell you how to behave; there may be an accepted code (Torah, Sharia, common law) which embodies the community's ideal.

The world is polarised into clear, simple black-and-white Good and Evil, and there is not the slightest doubt which is which. The Devil is as real as God: there is war in heaven (Rev. 12.7), which is reflected in wars on earth. Sin is a matter of acts and omissions. (Consideration of motives must await more sophisticated powers of perception. Abelard in the twelfth century was the first since New Testament times to introduce such subtlety into Christian moral theology.) Things are what they seem: 'reality' is what can be publicly shared—appearances. Even to want a private life is anti-social; one should have all things common. The peer group reigns supreme, and the unforgivable sins are dissent and non-conformity.

Communism elevates community into an ideology. Marx and Engels based their social theory about the 'classless society' on what they thought they had learnt from the works of Lewis Henry Morgan, whose *League of the Iroquois*, published in 1851, was a landmark in early anthropology. Morgan describes the Iroquois Indian confederacy of upstate New York, a federation of six little 'nations' whose total population never exceeded about 25,000. Thus what communism seeks to impose upon large, complex, developed societies is an ideal derived from, and appropriate to, small face-to-face communities bound together by ties of kinship and with the simplest of subsistence economies. In the last months of 1989 the industrialised nations of eastern Europe acknowledged with a shudder that it doesn't work. (Thus can abstract theory blind its adherents to reality: this is true of any 'ism', including the egalitarian idealism of liberal democracy.) Within a year, eastern Europe was already learning, the hard way, the ambiguities of a market economy.

Polarisation, which Marxism promotes in the form of 'class war', *is* an essential stage in coming to consciousness. It is involved in that aspect of our childhood training often referred to as socialisation. In order to form a socially acceptable personality, one must choose the Good and reject the Evil. The rejected, 'alien' aspects of human nature (aggression, undisciplined or deviant sexual impulses, slovenliness, laziness . . .) are either suppressed by a conscious ascetical effort which accepts the frustration and suffering involved, or else unconsciously repressed (that is, one is wholly unaware of the process). Repression may lead to neurotic symptoms in a way that suppression does not, but in either case the psyche is split into the conscious façade personality or persona, whose formation is essential to the functioning of society, and the unconscious (hence 'dark') shadow. 'A large part of education,' observes Neumann, will always be devoted to the formation of a persona, which will make the individual 'clean abut the house' and socially presentable, and which will teach him, not what is, but what may be regarded as, real; all human societies are at all times far more interested in instructing their members in the techniques of not looking, of overlooking and of looking the other way than in sharpening their observation, increasing their alertness and fostering their love of truth.[2]

It must be so, or we could not live together in society. It is a necessary stage which cannot be skipped, so (like the poor) it is always with us. The shadow, which conflicts with one's conscious values, cannot be acknowledged as part of oneself. It is therefore projected onto the outside world and is experienced as an external object to be fought and destroyed as 'the alien out there'.[3]

This is the answer to our Lord's question: 'Why beholdest thou the mote that is in thy brother's eye, but considerest not the beam that is in thine own eye?' (Matthew 7.3 AV). It is the real root of racism and of ethnic and religious and cultural conflict generally. It explains why attempts to combat racism are as divisive as racism itself, for to those who still need polarisation in order to feel secure, any kind of reconciliation *must* be subversive.

'For primitive man (continues Neumann)—and the mass man in every nation reacts like a primitive man—evil cannot be acknowledged as "his own evil" at all, since consciousness is still too weakly developed to be able to deal with the resulting conflict. It is for this reason that evil is invariably experienced by mass man as something alien, and the victims of shadow projection are therefore, always and everywhere, the aliens.'[4] The victim role is also projected onto the ethically inferior—criminals, psychopaths, drop-outs, inadequates—any who are unwilling or unable to measure up to the communal ideal. The superior, who have the temerity to rise *above* the collective average, are also victimised, for hatred of excellence (rooted in a mixture of envy and sloth) is a very powerful motive indeed in human affairs.

Group consciousness belongs to the tribal world in which pagan religion and magic are living realities, with their rituals, incantations and taboos. Those who have forgotten their own tribal past may refresh their memories by consulting Iona and Peter Opie's *The Lore and Language of Schoolchildren*.[5]

* * *

The world of the natural community is that of Israel in the Promised Land: a stable, structured kinship community with shared traditions and culture, in a land they could call their own. It took a long time to establish.

Not all the Hebrews went down into Egypt. Not all who did took the long way back with Moses and Joshua. Some, notably of the tribes of Judah and Simeon, seem to have drifted back up from the south through the Negev to settle in the area around Beersheba, Hebron and Bethlehem. But as we have seen, it is those who did go down into Egypt and who experienced the Exodus, the Covenant at Sinai and the forty years in the desert who become the carriers of the national consciousness. It is their story which is adopted by all the tribes as their own.

The Joseph tribes, Ephraim and Manasseh, enter the land from the east and (leaving behind Reuben, Gad, and part of Manasseh in the Trans-Jordan) work their way up past Jericho and Ai to settle in the hill country of Ephraim from Bethel to Shechem and what will later become Samaria. It is they who form the core of the northern kingdom when Israel separates from Judah after the death of Solomon.

When the children of Israel cross the Jordan, Moses does not go with them: his parental task is done. But before a stable society under a Hebrew monarchy is established, a long period of turbulence and anarchy lies ahead for the semi-nomads, still dependent on charismatic leadership as they begin to put down roots.

The agricultural revolution into the settled life of village and town is as traumatic a phase of human history as the urban revolution which uproots people. Not everyone is capable of settling down: the Australian Aborigine must go walkabout, the gipsy must remain a traveller, and we all know the 'rolling stone' and the perpetual student. Some people are incapable of commitment; many a marriage breakdown is rooted in psychic unsuitability for marriage in the first place. But rootedness is an essential stage of formation for those who keep on growing. Hence the Benedictine vow of stability, which enabled the Benedictines to play no small part in transforming tribal Europe into the settled civilisation of the Middle Ages.

The crucial invention of the agricultural revolution is the plough. With hoe-agriculture, you must move on every few years as the shallow soil becomes exhausted. The deep-cutting plough makes possible the cultivation of the heavier soils of the fertile valleys, proper turning over of the soil, and the ploughing in of fallow crops. With crop rotation, the same fields can be cultivated indefinitely. *You don't need to move on.* It becomes worth while to build permanent houses and temples, protecting walls, and irrigation systems. The food surplus can support a larger population and at a higher standard of living, with specialised craftsmen and organised trade. The symbol of settled agriculture in the Bible is not the annual crops of wheat and barley but the vine, which requires years of patient cultivation before it bears fruit (1 Kings 4.25).

It takes a couple of centuries for the Hebrews to settle down. The Book of Judges recounts their failure to dislodge the original inhabitants of the land, and the exploits of the charismatic strong men (and women!) of the Dark Age when every man does what is right in his own eyes. Many a political leader in our own time has Samuel's problem of finding a transcendent loyalty to keep rival tribes or factions or ethnic groups from flying at one another's throats. The common shrine at Shiloh proves inadequate. As so often, it is the threat of an external foe that finally induces the warring tribes to unite under a king. Even then, Saul's authority is threatened by the growing popularity of the new charismatic leader, David, who during his years as an outcast (1 Samuel 21–30) reverts to the semi-nomadic Habiru way of life.

David is a Judean and rules at first from Hebron. But he sees the need for a tribally neutral capital and achieves it by capturing the Jebusite stronghold of Jerusalem, complete with cult and culture. The Jebusites were not driven out (Judges 1.21). David and his followers simply moved in among them and took over, learning from them Canaanite techniques of civil administration and religious practice.

There, on the holy hill of Zion, David installs the Ark of the Covenant. Without the stability of that little walled city and its sanctuary as a focus of the worship of Yahweh, the Israelites would probably have been assimilated into Canaanite civilisation and their unique vocation would have been lost. The prophets' denunciations make clear how close they came to losing their identity, despite the reforms of Hezekiah and Josiah. Assimilationist and separatist factions were to remain at loggerheads through the time of Nehemiah and Ezra, the Samaritan schism, the Maccabean revolt and the Essene schism, down to the Sadducees and Pharisees of our Lord's time. They are still with us in modern Jewry, not least in Israel, where the gulf between secular and religious Jews seems well-nigh unbridgeable.

David's personal life won't bear too close inspection, and the actual extent of his empire appears to have been rather less impressive than tradition gives him credit for.[6] Nevertheless, he is idealised as the type of perfect kingship, to which Israel will look back with longing. It is the throne of David that the Messiah is to inherit.

Solomon is a younger son who comes to the throne through palace intrigue. He disposes of his rivals in time-honoured sticky manner, and proceeds to enhance his glory.

Traditional Middle Eastern kingship was, and is, on the pattern of the Bedouin sheikh rather than that of the oriental despot. It is kingship on a human scale, and its essence is availability to all one's subjects. The pattern can be seen in Exodus 18, where the people bring all their grievances to Moses. It is the ageing David's neglect of 'sitting in the gate' which gives Absalom his chance to 'steal the hearts of the people' (2 Samuel 15.1–6).

Alas, Solomon prefers the imperial model of kingship, after the Egyptian and Phoenician fashion. History plays into his hands, for Egypt and Mesopotamia, the superpowers of the day, seem both to be weak at the same time. In the resulting power-vacuum, Solomon is seen building a far-flung commercial empire, sealed by a marriage alliance with Egypt and a trade treaty with the king of Tyre. Religious syncretism develops apace.

Bureaucracy also flourishes, especially in Solomon's Ministry of Building and Public Works (1 Kings 4 and 5). Forced-labour levies, murderous taxation, and ostentatious luxury at court (1 Kings 9 and 10) prove more than the economy can carry, even with such advanced industrial developments as copper-mining and smelting. When Solomon turns to military expenditure, an able young civil servant named Jeroboam rebels. Solomon tries to buy his loyalty with promotion, but in vain: this is the Jeroboam who will wrest most of the kingdom from Solomon's son (1 Kings 11.26–40).

From David's capture of Jerusalem around 1000 BC to Solomon's death is barely seventy years, after which the kingdom splits into two. Those seventy years are remembered as the Hebrew Golden Age, and 'Solomon and his glory' joins the idealised King David in the gallery of national heroes.

And there *is* glory in Jerusalem: the little walled city itself, the royal palace, the temple and its liturgy. This is the age of the psalms praising Yahweh's victory over his foes. It all helps to form and focus the corporate identity of the people of God, shaping the community's world-view from within the ordered cosmos of the seemingly unconquerable City of God. The Chosen People are at last enjoying their Promised Land. For one brief moment in their troubled history, they know what it is to exact tribute instead of paying it. That glorious memory, enhanced by nostalgia, will sustain them through all their later wanderings.

But the cost has to be reckoned. The achievements of the few are always made possible by the many: no one lives or works independently of the culture and economy of his time and place. So long as there is a sense of community, so long as the people feel that they 'belong', they *expect* a representative few to stand in high places and achieve great things on behalf of all; the hero is a recognised role. (It is still so today in the world of sport.) There is no sense of alienation from what one does not happen personally to share or even understand. One takes pride in the achievements of members of the community more gifted or more fortunate than oneself. The effort is a communal effort; the achievement, a communal achievement.

But when a sense of community is lacking—because part of the population feel unfairly excluded, or because (with a breakdown of authority) the community itself has become fragmented into mutually hostile groups, or because (as happens in all empires and in modern industrial societies) the community has simply become *too large* for real human relationships—then the privileged are hated. Their achievements become the object not of communal pride but of collective envy, and their cost is resented as 'exploitation'.

This is how 'middle-class' has come in modern times to be a pejorative term. The middle classes have always been the backbone of any civilisation (the word referred originally to the culture of the small city state) and of town life generally, as distinct from agricultural peasant societies. Indeed, one of the third world's greatest problems today is precisely the *lack* of a substantial middle class between the over-wealthy few (usually large landowners) at the top and the impoverished many: the lack of those skilled craftsmen, shopkeepers and traders, teachers and doctors and other professionals (nowadays including technicians, accountants, civil servants, engineers) whose skill and diligence sustain town and city life. But with industrialisation and the drift off the land into huge conurbations, the civilised city turns for the majority into a concrete jungle, and the Marxist class war is born.

The exploitation which begins under Solomon (1 Kings 5.13–18; 9.20–23) is intensified under the inept Rehoboam, who (like one or two English kings who are better forgotten) prefers the approval of his flattering peer-group to the wise counsel of elder statesmen (1 Kings 12). Jeroboam's revolt focusses a tribalism that is surfacing again anyway, and the bulk of the tribes break away to form a separate community, the northern kingdom of Israel.

With the fertile plain of Jezreel, and astride the main trade routes, Israel prospers and becomes sophisticated and cosmopolitan. The southern kingdom of Judah, economically poorer but Jerusalem-centred, survives longer and becomes the custodian of both written and oral tradition, including that brought to Jerusalem by refugees from the north when Samaria falls to the Assyrians in 722 BC.

The Pentateuch as we know it took shape in the Exile, when there was need of a meaningful past in order to make the present endurable and the future possible. The Jerusalem-centred chronicles of I and II Samuel and I and II Kings rarely mention Abraham or Moses. But the destruction of Jerusalem called for a new model of the past, stressing Abraham and his seed and the Exodus from Egypt. This need must already have been acutely felt in the northern kingdom as soon as it cut itself off from Jerusalem and its Davidic traditions—to which, in any case, the northern tribes had never been more than loosely attached.

Levites fleeing southward in 722 brought their northern traditions with them, and these were probably put together in some form in the time of Hezekiah (716–687 BC). Lost or hidden during the reign of the apostate Manasseh (687–642 BC), this Book of the Covenant (the core of what we know as Deuteronomy) is rediscovered, or brought out of hiding, in 621 BC under Josiah (2 Kings 22). The king is shocked to learn its contents, which seem to be new to him: if it is true (and the prophetess Huldah confirms that it is), the people of God are in grave danger of losing their identity. It is now, at the king's command, that the annual celebration of the Passover in Jerusalem begins, 'for no such passover had been kept since the days of the judges who judged Israel, or during all the days of the kings of Israel or the kings of Judah; but in the eighteenth year of King Josiah this passover was kept to the Lord in Jerusalem' (2 Kings 23.21–23).

* * *

A community defines itself by contrast with outsiders, with those who *don't* belong. Brotherly love (*philia*) is exercised toward insiders and kith-and-kin, who alone are recognised as fully human; xenophobia toward strangers and opters-out. Aliens must either assimilate or stay in a ghetto—or be driven out, with all the horrors of 'ethnic cleansing'. *A community cannot tolerate internal diversity.* Only a *koinonia* can do that—a fellowship with a shared ultimate loyalty transcending communal diversities. In a community, as with the individual, internal conflicts are projected onto external 'enemies'.

Communal consciousness is always strengthened in time of war, especially one that can be proclaimed a 'just' or 'holy' war. (The Christian Crusades are the mirror image of the Islamic *jihad*.) War is natural to childhood. In peacetime the same function is served by the identification of scapegoats. A natural community *needs* enemies and outcasts in order to be itself. This is the root of racism. It is why untouchability dies so hard in India: the cleansing of 'lepers' (another of the messianic signs) is no more welcome than the opening of the eyes of the blind. Those bloodthirsty psalms extolling vengeance on the enemies of Yahweh belong here. (Of course they are 'sub-Christian'! So is a large part of the personality of every one of us. The reason why they make us squirm is that they are entirely too close to the bone.)

The idealised kingdom of David and Solomon is the

model aspired to by medieval Christendom. The culturally homogeneous community under the law of God remains the ideal of Orthodox Judaism and of Islam to this day.

But the New Testament Gospel is not proclaimed to Israel-in-the-Promised Land. Until she has been through the shattering experience of exile and dispersion, she is only formed, not transformed. She is too complacently at ease in Zion. The good news for her is of judgement—on Israel herself, not on her foes, who are even seen as instruments of God's will—by a righteous and holy God who cares enough about his people to chastise them in order to restore them to right relationship with himself.

The world of community is the childhood world of heroes and villains like cowboys and Indians, cops and robbers. It is a world of epic poetry and legend and story-telling around the campfire, of kings and queens and knights in shining armour and fair ladies, of walled towns and village life, of ethnic religion and established churches, of tradition and hierarchy and political stability, of temples and shrines and festivals, of priesthood and liturgy, sacrament and ceremonial, of myth and symbol, of patriotism and pageantry, of music, dance and drama.

It is also the world of communal responsibility, in which the widow and the orphan, the aged and the handicapped are cared for by the kinship-group. Deuteronomy 15.4-5 hopefully promises that 'there will be no poor among you . . . if only you will obey the voice of the Lord your God'. With greater realism the same passage concludes (v. 11) 'the poor will never cease out of the land; therefore I command you, You shall open your hand to your brother, to the needy and to the poor'. It was this tribal sense of corporate responsibility which so impressed Engels and Marx in Lewis Henry Morgan's description of the Iroquois Indian community. What they did not realise is that it can only operate freely (i.e. without coercive structures to enforce it) in societies small enough for face-to-face relationships.

Most of us live much of our lives on the 'closed community' level of consciousness, centred in the layer of our personality formed in childhood. Its reassuring code morality is necessary both to the formation of consciousness and as a breakwater against emotional chaos in times of stress. It remains permanently valid for a large part of the human race. Very many are genuinely unable, in this life, to venture beyond the security of the closed community and its certainties. For those who have never experienced a satisfactory integration with a mother-figure, conventional roles and 'masks' are absolutely essential to hide the emptiness within. For such, with no clear boundaries to their own personality, any kind of personal encounter apart from a safe role is perilous. For them, a 'green pasture' where sheep may safely graze may be a permanent necessity, unless or until their emotional crippling at the infant level can be healed. But many others, who ought to move on, prefer to settle down into conventional respectability and so to evade the moral effort of becoming a responsible individual.

Formation through belonging in a community is essential to being human. But the Christian disciple ought not to be content to stop growing at this point, for those whose identity remains dependent on the natural community of 'our own kind' will never be able to love their enemies or the stranger in their midst, nor to welcome diversity, to practise *agapē* or to experience *koinonia*.

Medieval Christendom was as confident as Israel in her Promised Land, belligerent and ruthless against the Muslim infidel without and also, alas, against the Christian heretic and the alien Jew within. Traditional Catholic theology is rooted in the 'walled city' of Christendom, within which all belong as a matter of course. It is at this stage that the 'Purgative Way' of traditional Christian spirituality is most relevant, with its concentration on purification from sin and resisting evil. This kind of asceticism presupposes a communal culture in which sin and virtue, good and evil, are clearly defined and unambiguously recognisable.

Calvinist and Lutheran theology at first envisaged a

Protestant alternative Christendom, equally intolerant of nonconformity. *Cuius regio, eius religio*: at the time of the Reformation, one's religion was emphatically not a matter of personal choice; subjects were expected to follow the religion of their ruler. But once the monolithic unity was broken, it was only a matter of time before the authority of the individual conscience would assert itself. So it was with Israel after the division of the kingdom.

9
Exile

For those who keep on growing, the next transformation is that which is normal to adolescence in societies in which personal decision-making is expected of adults. A period of psychological detachment from the community, for those who have experienced its formative 'belonging' and are ready to move on, is necessary for the emergence of mature individuals capable of personal responsibility and initiative.

The human race is divided into those who see things and persons mainly from the outside and those who can also see them from within. Both ways of seeing are needed if we are to be safe and sane: to see only from the outside is dangerously naïve; to see only from within is, for an adult, psychotic. (Much mental illness can be described as the eruption into an adult mind of states of consciousness and modes of perception characteristic of infancy.) Each way of seeing, by itself, excludes part of reality. Broadly speaking, to see from the outside is the way of scientific observation; to see from within is the way of personal experience.

Insiders see things from the outside: reality is what can be publicly shared. Things are what they seem; there are no ambiguities. The landmarks are familiar, and you know where you are. Children need this kind of security, so responsible parents *must* defend stability and order.

Outsiders see things from within: they see through the appearances, polite fictions, hypocrisies and self-deceptions of society. (Elijah, the archetypal prophet of ancient Israel, is an outsider from the Trans-Jordan; the later prophets, too, are sufficiently detached from the consensus of their community to see what is really happening and where it is inexorably leading.) We are born outsiders and are brought inside the communal consciousness through socialisation. Small children are still devastatingly honest, until they learn the price of approval.

The contrast between traditional and modern societies emerges at adolescence. Tribal initiation makes you fully an insider. Most tribal people never need to think for themselves, and indeed in such societies no one of less than heroic stature can achieve independence of thought and action. But modern civilisation presupposes individuality. You cannot run factories and hospitals and power stations and universities and transport systems and scientific research on the basis of ancestral custom. Bus drivers and computer programmers and surgeons and shop stewards and civil servants and engineers and bankers and technicians must act predictably (according to a rational plan), impartially (neither favouring kin nor taking bribes) and without having either to consult the omens or participate in a palaver every time a decision has to be made.

So those who live in modern societies, or wherever the influence of Western civilisation is felt, are increasingly called to become outsiders for a time in order to become authentic persons. In our societies, responsible adolescents *must* rebel. It is a second dragon-slaying. (With us, the initiation-*into* stage is pushed back to the start of primary school.)

The new time of turmoil is forced upon us by the onset of puberty. The matter-of-fact childhood observation that the human race comes in two shapes turns into a disturbing awareness that the opposite sex really is 'other'. As we explore the possibilities of real personal relationships (as distinct from role-play) we embark upon the long process of discovering that there is in every human being, including ourself, an inner core of integrity which can never be shared, even in marriage. We learn the inescapable loneliness of being a person.

Our stable childhood world is shattered as, with growing perception, we begin to see through its certainties and the advertised motives of the adult world. Things, and people, are *not* what they seem.

There is an attractive mythology about mother love and family life which is still widely accepted at its face value, especially by the older generation. It was taken for granted by traditional moral theology, which is one of the reasons why that discipline has needed rethinking. It's what we all want to believe: children, because they need security above all else; parents, because otherwise they'd have to face some unpalatable truths about themselves. The community takes for granted that kinship and proximity automatically establish 'bonds of natural affection'. You don't have to go to the magistrate's court to learn otherwise, only to the nursery. Closer attention to folklore and fairy tale would reveal that no villain is more feared than the wicked *step*-mother: not even a fairy tale can openly admit that one's *own* mother—the very source of life, on whom the child is totally dependent—might also be the source of the terror.

Not even Freud could acknowledge that, probably because of his deep and unrecognised attachment to his own mother.[1] He talked of revolt against the father, but did not (as popularly supposed) advocate it. He recognised only too clearly the indispensable function of paternal authority in disciplining into civilised channels the demonic energies of the 'maternal' unconscious, and he clung neurotically to that authority in both his public and private life. It was his inability to relinquish his 'paternal' authority that led to his break with Jung, who had been Freud's protégé and heir apparent as leader of the psychoanalytic movement.[2] Freud sensed the perils-of-soul, should the revolt against reason ever succeed and the flood-gates be opened to the 'black tide' of unreason, which for him included, above all, religion. It was as a bulwark against this terror that he promulgated his celebrated doctrine about sex.[3] He wanted to reduce the unconscious to a decayed consciousness (made up entirely of once-conscious things that had been repressed) which could be explained in terms of the mechanistic cause-and-effect thinking which dominated the science of his day. Jung saw the unconscious as living and creative and a potential source of wisdom; for Freud, the unconscious (which he had himself let out of Pandora's box) proved too great a threat to his own ordered cosmos to be allowed real autonomy.

Jung ventured further into the psychic hinterland and identified the menace as the Terrible Mother of mythology. His own revolt against the conventional religion of his parson-father closely parallels that of many young people today.[4] Jung widened and deepened both the concept of the unconscious and our awareness of its cultural importance. But even he drew back when he felt his European individuality threatened by tribal consciousness while living for a time in Africa.[5]

In recent years the existentialists have publicised their experience of the abyss which underlies the purely natural when seen in alienation from God. But it's all there in Genesis 1. We like to get to the bottom of things, but in the natural realm there is no bottom to things. At the bottom of everything, God—*and without God, no bottom to anything.* It takes courage to face that with integrity, which is why there are so few genuine atheists. Nietzsche cracked under the strain. Bertrand Russell didn't, but his failure to find the mathematical certainty he sought turned one of the most brilliant minds that has ever lived from a philosophical optimist into a sceptic and almost destroyed him as a man.[6] Sartre sought assurance in the substitute faith of Marxism.

Using existentialist insights, some recent psychologists have traced the terror of the abyss to its source in an inverted, negative *eros* between infant and mother—the very place where sentiment and society alike see, and demand to see, the image of security.[7] In the place of *eros*, there is fear. (The love that casts out fear is not *eros* but *agapē*.) There is ambiguity at the roots of life.

The tension between the role-play expected by the community and the adolescent's inner experience lies at the bottom of the gulf between the generations. Conventional behaviour is imposed on children as the price of approval, as it must be in any civilised society. Above all, one is expected to behave *as if* one feels 'natural affection' for kith and kin, whether this is in fact the case or not. Sometimes, wonderfully, it is. If not, one can be brainwashed into believing the charade oneself for years. One desperately *wants* to believe it, for where else is security to be found?

Then one day one's inner integrity rebels. One drops the mask, opts out of the role of dutiful son or daughter, and the long-repressed self begins at last to emerge. You do your own thing.

People are shocked. Parents are bewildered and hurt at one's lack of gratitude.

Gratitude? For years in hell, or at best in a limbo of non-communication?

Polite society is very frightened. So was Adam in the garden, when he hid himself from the Lord God because he knew he was naked. Not for nothing is the opening of the eyes of the blind the first of the signs of the Messiah. Polite society crucified the Messiah.

Is it love to keep up a pretence, to live a lie? How does one discern at what point, and in what manner, one must—for her own sake—shatter the illusions of a yearning mother? *Agapē* must be prepared not only to endure suffering but also, on occasion, knowingly to cause it. The first we see in the Cross; the second, in our Lord's relationships with his own family and friends.

The illusions would not exist if communication had not got blocked. For some, communication never gets started: in countless families it is already blocked before any child is born. The agonising consequences of this situation were brilliantly dramatised in the John Hopkins quartet of BBC television plays, *Talking to a Stranger*,[8] in which the root of the alienation lay in the refusal of both parents to accept the reality of suffering in their own childhood.

We love because we are first loved; also we sin because we are first sinned against: here is solidarity indeed! We all bear the scars. Because the primal relationship is one of total dependence, it is necessarily ambivalent: every withdrawal of the all-providing maternal presence, every 'hiding of the face', *must* fill the infant with anxiety and fear.

The ambivalence cannot be avoided, so long as human beings are born helpless. It can of course be denied, as it is by those who make to themselves gods of social and political theories appropriate to a perfect world, which must then be *made* to work, at whatever cost, in the real world. We are all wounded persons, all of us to some extent misshapen, which is why the theories never do work. None of us starts from scratch. 'Original sin' (or 'original suffering'?) is transmitted by psychic contagion from wounded parent to vulnerable child in the very relationship that makes us human. It is part of the human condition, and there are no exemptions. Anxiety and frustration are as inherent in growth as desire and striving: the wish to be without them is nostalgia for the womb.

But the wish is there. It is the passive temptation: the line of least resistance, of effortless drifting, of apathy.

The active temptation is to try to evade both human finitude and human sinfulness: 'Ye shall be as gods' (Genesis 3.5). So we were, once, in the infant universe we knew so well how to manipulate. That paradisal memory, with its fantasies of innocent omnipotence, underlies all utopian thinking, from Pelagius to Rousseau, socialism, anarchism, and the Great American Dream.

Loss of innocence is the first and inescapable step on the long road to sanctity. Much traditional spirituality confused the two. True sanctity lies on the far side of the struggle with doubt and temptation. Jesus of Nazareth the full-grown man is indeed sinless, but he is not innocent. He knows far more about temptation than we do, for he alone has felt its full force: he alone resisted to the end. We give in.

It is in adolescence that the innocence of childhood normally drops away. The old boundaries and cultural landmarks crumble, and new ones have not yet emerged to contain and order the chaos of sense-experience, which is now encountered 'raw' (as in the strident sounds and garish lights of the disco) with an immediacy we have not known since infancy.

Adolescence is our second age of ambiguity. In the first, as toddlers, we veer between the joy of our new-found independence and rushing back to Mummy at the first fright. Now, amid the exhilaration of adventure and exploration, we are torn between idealism and disillusionment. We see through adult pretensions but have not yet had to cope with adult responsibilities. We see through the Establishment, but have not yet perceived the perils to contain which Establishments must be painstakingly evolved. As students we spend whole nights arguing about how *we* are going to put the world right. As ordinary teenagers we crave the 'togetherness' of the coffee bar, the anti-adult conformity of the peer group, the tribal music and dance. Yet there is also the new need of privacy for day-dreaming and mooning about, for writing poetry, for pondering the insights (as old as man) which burst upon each new generation with the force of revelation. Until we can transcend ourself sufficiently to stand back and reflect, we are not yet fully conscious. Distance is necessary for perspective, and that means a measure of solitude.

Modern psychology since Freud has tended to stress the importance of the capacity for intimate personal relationships as the source of health and happiness and the test of emotional maturity. But there are other ways to fulfilment, which many find in absorption in their work. As Anthony Storr points out in his recent book *Solitude*,[9] the capacity to be alone is also a sign of maturity. Indeed, solitude is essential for the exercise of creative imagination; thinking is a solitary activity even when other people are present. Emotional maturity depends not only on experience of secure attachment to an identity-figure, but also on the capacity to discover and express our true feelings and to trust the authenticity of our own perceptions, as distinct from what others project upon us or expect of us.

Solitude promotes insight, which is why those who take their discipleship seriously commonly practise some form of periodic 'retreat' into silence and recollection, either alone or in company with others. Such temporary withdrawal from the distractions and responsibilities of daily life enables one to see things in perspective (as an artist from time to time stands back from concentration on details in order to see the work as a whole); one is thus better able to consider and perhaps re-order one's priorities. Our daily prayer time is a sort of mini-retreat.

It is in adolescence that we should begin seriously to explore who we are and what life is all about. It is not easy in the pervasive noise and lack of privacy of modern life. Indeed, many are only too glad to evade the necessity to think. But with the collapse of childhood certainties, we are inescapably faced with the anxiety of freedom and of moral choices which are far from obvious, and with the risks of responsibility. It is the age of existentialism. For those who dare to think, everything is now questioned: who am I? who are you? *is* there a God? what is man? how do we know anything? is there any meaning to life?—and if not, how can one find what Paul Tillich calls 'the courage to *be*'?

Some fail to find it and fall into nihilism and despair. If there is no meaning in life, if there is nothing to live *for*, why bother to live? Large numbers of young folk are simply bored, robbed by premature sophistication of childhood's capacity for wonder and by the mass media of the ability to devise their own amusements. Why *not* give oneself up, infant-fashion, to sensation in the present moment? What else *is* there? Why *not* seek ecstasy and oblivion through drink or drugs?

Such regression has always been a temptation for the bewildered, especially for any with a tendency to depression. The temptation is all the greater amid the increasing stresses of modern life, not least those generated by the mass media, which keep the glittering possibilities of the consumer society before the eyes of those who (through lack of ability or lack of opportunity or both) will never be able to achieve them. Unreal expectations are as potent a cause of despair as actual poverty.

But there is a deeper reason for the vulnerability of the

young in the late twentieth century, and that is the prolonged psychic earthquake which has shattered the foundations of Western civilisation. It first broke the surface in the French Revolution, but because Napoleon met his Waterloo the shock waves didn't really penetrate the dominant culture until the First World War. Christendom was buried in Flanders' Fields, together with the potential leaders of an entire generation. The poet Yeats saw the devastating implications of that spiritual vacuum:

> Things fall apart; the centre cannot hold;
> Mere anarchy is loosed upon the world,
> The blood-dimmed tide is loosed, and everywhere
> The ceremony of innocence is drowned;
> The best lack all conviction, while the worst
> Are full of passionate intensity.[10]

At the end of the Second World War the culture shock which began with the discovery of Auschwitz and Belsen reached a sudden blinding climax at Hiroshima on the Feast of the Transfiguration in 1945. It was not only 75,000 Japanese lives that were blasted that summer day, but the continuity of history, the credibility of morality, and all the liberal assumptions about rationality and human goodness. Auschwitz and Hiroshima laid bare the nihilism behind the mask of a civilisation that still widely practised the Christian religion but had almost wholly abandoned the Christian faith.

Jeff Nuttall, writing in 1968 (the year in which, as he puts it, the young made war on their elders), describes that culture shock from within.[11] VE night, he says, took place in one world and VJ night in another. The European victory over Hitler confirmed the old values of community and family and nation: 'We knew the Devil and had killed him.' But the Japanese victory was achieved at the cost of alienating all the values confirmed in the first victory: 'We had espoused an evil as great as the Nazi genocide (and) a monstrous uncertainty both of future and of morality. . . . If we also were wrong, who was ever right? If no one was right, what was right, and was right anyway relevant?' What could guide us through this new and terrifying freedom?

We had lost our collective innocence, and all institutions—church, political party, social class, happy family—had been stripped of moral authority. 'No longer could teacher, magistrate, politician, don, or even loving parent guide the young. Their membership of the H-bomb society automatically cancelled anything they might have to say on questions of right and wrong.'

But not all recognised this, and a gulf opened between those who saw, and those who did not see, the implications of the mushroom cloud.

> The people who had passed puberty at the time of the bomb found that they were incapable of conceiving of life *without* a future. Their patterns of habit had formed—the steady job, the pension, the mortgage, the insurance policy, personal savings, support and respect for the protection of the law, all the paraphernalia of constructive, secure family life. They had learned their game and it was the only game they knew. To acknowledge the truth of their predicament would be to abandon the whole pattern of their lives. They would therefore have to pretend . . .
>
> The people who had not yet reached puberty at the time of the bomb were incapable of conceiving life *with* a future. . . . Dad was a liar. He lied about the war and he lied about sex. He lied about the bomb and he lied about the future. He lived his life on an elaborate system of pretence that had been going on for hundreds of years. The so-called 'generation gap' started then and has been increasing ever since.

Those not yet fully initiated into membership of the community suddenly saw, with the devastating clarity of the small child, the dark underside of our civilisation—and recoiled in stunned horror. For a time the Campaign for Nuclear Disarmament offered hope of real change, but with the failure of that last desperate appeal by the young to their elders on the basis of the latter's own professed belief in the primacy of reason and conscience, the disillusionment was total. 'The decline of the anti-bomb movement in 1962 left us stranded with the unbearable,' says Nuttall.[12]

The young saw through the hypocrisy of governments that ignored in practice the morality they preached and enforced. They perceived in the society around them a hidden death-wish.

Of the rise of pop culture during those years Nuttall observes that its clashing colours and raucous sounds 'were the very aesthetic of the severed nerve, for our nerves *were* severed, severed from certainty, severed from social and family warmth, and above all severed from future. We were stranded with our sensations, and our sensations screamed, and we recognised the aesthetic of the scream.' The older generation, meantime, for the most part could not hear jazz. ('They said it was cacophony, and they meant it.')

'So we knew where we stood,' says Nuttall. 'Not one of us had any serious political preoccupation or any belief in the changeability of society and events. No single solitary one amongst us had the slightest spark of hope or gave a damn about a thing except the crackling certainty of Now.'[13]

It was then, he observes, that teenagers became incapable of thinking more than half an hour ahead: of what use to speak of promises, responsible undertakings, honour, principles, to minds so conditioned? Drugs enhance the sensations of the moment; dangers such as addiction or death belong to a future too improbable to be taken seriously. Sick humour (in which values are totally rejected), once a sign of certifiable madness, is embraced in a deliberate attack on a society that has betrayed life. Ritual violence is enacted to exorcise pent-up aggression. Taboos are confronted and broken. Young drug-takers deliberately try to dissolve the self in order to escape from a reality too painful to bear.

There is still much of this in today's drug sub-culture. The world has moved on since the 1960s; at the very least, there still *is* a world. And there is an admirable new post-

Bomb generation many of whom devote themselves with energy and enthusiasm to causes such as human rights, famine relief, nuclear disarmament and environmental concerns—mostly with a healthy scepticism of such established adult institutions as political parties or trade unions. But the Bomb is still there and, in addition, enough young people see no way of escape from the meaninglessness and boredom of the consumer society, or from the sordid urban poverty of those excluded from it, to provide a burgeoning market for the traffickers in heroin, cocaine, and crack.

* * *

Human individuality[14] is a tremendous achievement, and it is very costly. 'God himself cannot liberate man from his aloneness,' says Tillich.

> It is man's greatness that he is centred on himself. Separated from his world, he is thus able to look at it. Only because he can look at it can he know and love and transform it. God, in creating him ruler of the earth, had to separate him and thrust him into aloneness. Man is also therefore able to be spoken to, by God and by man. He can ask questions, and give answers, and make decisions. He has freedom, for good and evil. Only he who has an impenetrable centre in himself is free. Only he who is alone can claim to be a man. This is the greatness and the burden of man.[15]

The transforming crisis of adolescence happens naturally in modern urban societies, but it can be forced upon whole peoples without their consent or expectation. This happened to the children of Israel in the Exile, with the collapse of their old certainties. It happens wherever people from traditional societies drift into modern cities. It happens wherever war, famine, persecution or economic change uproots communities and disperses them as migrants or refugees. It happened in England in the religious and political upheavals of the seventeenth century and later in the industrial revolution. (The immense popularity of Bunyan's *Pilgrim's Progress* in the late seventeenth century was due to its providing a map of the Way of discipleship for those who felt lost without the old communal guidance.) In his book *The Unprivileged*[16] Jeremy Seabrook describes the detribalisation of his own Anglo-Saxon clan in rural Northamptonshire within his own memory. His vivid portrayal of the English tribal mind from within illuminates the situation of many a family in the back streets, housing estates and new towns of Britain.

Detribalisation brings great perils-of-soul but also, for those who persevere through the crisis of spiritual adolescence, immense and exhilarating new possibilities.

It is at the point of detribalisation that evangelism takes on its full urgency. All religions strengthen community: that is part of their function. Only the Christian Gospel insists that you are accepted by God *even if outcast from community*. Any religion or none will do for the insider; the Christian Gospel is the only good news there is for the outsider, the outcast and the scapegoat.

* * *

The promise to Abraham doesn't end with the Promised Land: it includes the mission to all nations. With the wisdom of hindsight, we can see that the people of God have to move on. It doesn't seem like that to them at the time. The far-seeing Jeremiah is arrested as a traitor when he proclaims as the will of God for Israel that they should submit to the king of Babylon and settle down in exile.

The destruction of the seemingly unconquerable city of Jerusalem and of the temple of the Lord marks the 'end of the world' for those who have put their trust in Mount Zion. It is the end of their ordered cosmos, the tearing down of the psychic as well as material walls that have kept chaos at bay. It is the mother and father of culture shocks. How deeply the erstwhile nomads have become indigenised in Canaan is seen in the psalmist's complaint (137.4 AV): 'How shall we sing the Lord's song in a strange land?'

The desolation of the Hebrew exiles is due not merely to

contemporary notions of the territoriality of deity, according to which if you leave your god's land, you are cut off from your god. It is due also to their own psychic disorientation, for when you become rooted in the soil, you lose the nomad's adaptability.

But this transforming shock is the necessary next step in the discipleship of the people of God. The Exodus uproots them from being an unstructured collective embedded in their environment; the Exile, from being a structured community in their own sacral nation-state. Both 'deaths' are necessary preludes to life on new levels of consciousness. The Exodus is the birth of the people of God, their expulsion from the womb into dependence on an all-providing parental figure, from which they are weaned by the death of Moses and their entry into Canaan. The Exile corresponds to the upheaval of adolescence, when we leave the 'land flowing with milk and honey' of childhood, learn to accept personal responsibility, and become at least capable of personal discipleship.

10
Dispersion

The next integration is the individuality taken for granted by modern civilisation: the stable adult ego, capable of personal initiative, responsibility and self-discipline, whose identity is centred in reflective rational consciousness. At the beginning of the seventeenth century Descartes sets the tone: 'I *think*; therefore I am.'

We are now able to enter into personal relationships which are not mere role-play. We can meet other persons *as* 'other' without feeling threatened by their otherness. We no longer require the support of a homogeneous culture, but are able to tolerate and even to rejoice in the diversity of a plural society. The ideal is now that brotherly love (*philia*) should be exercised toward *all*, not just to those who belong to one's own community. This is the point of the parable of the Good Samaritan, told by Jesus to a lawyer who wants to establish manageable limits to his obligation (Luke 10.25–37).

We are now capable of abstract, logical thought. The archetypal image is displaced by the idea, which (in Neumann's words) 'is regarded as a conscious content to which one can, though one need not, take up an attitude. Instead of being possessed by an archetype, we now "have an idea" or, better still, "pursue an idea".'[1] We enjoy the cut-and-thrust of debate and do not feel personally threatened by criticism of our ideas; we may in fact be good friends with those who hold opposing views.

Rational thought and personal responsibility are taken for granted by the political theory of modern constitutional states, in which citizenship is a legal status having no necessary connection with kinship or culture. We are now in the world of contractual relationships and of bureaucratic organisation. Genuine democracy (with one-man-one-vote, the secret ballot, and real choice) presupposes individuality.

There is a link between individuality and literacy: whereas the non-literate must depend on oral tradition, the literate is free to develop an independent point of view. (He does not, of course, necessarily choose to do so.) One of the first acts of authoritarian regimes is to impose censorship on the written word.

The conventional wisdom is that it was in the Renaissance of the fifteenth century that modern European individuality was born, together with perspective in art (which implies a personal point of view). It was certainly then that the invention of printing enabled the rapid dissemination of ideas, including those of the Protestant Reformation with its stress on the sovereignty of the individual conscience before God. The translation of the Bible—by Luther into German, by Calvin into French, and by Tyndale and Coverdale into English—had a profoundly formative influence on those vernacular languages and hence also on the European mind. The articulate consciousness of an entire culture shifted onto the new plane. It was of course at first a minority culture. Change is always initiated by creative minorities.

Renaissance consciousness gradually spread through Western society with the spread of literacy, down to about the time of the French Revolution. Since then, creative minorities have tended to lead the Romantic revolt against Renaissance values. By the late twentieth century, with the spread of the mass media (especially radio and television, which do not require literacy) we could be said to have come to the end of Renaissance Man.

But there was an earlier renaissance, in the twelfth century, without which that of the fifteenth would have been impossible.

Our European civilisation has had one immense advantage over every previous one: we didn't have to start from scratch. In the Dark Ages, Christian monks (almost the only literates left in the West) copied and preserved not only the Bible and early Christian writings but also the secular classical literature on which pagan education had been based. (Very few actual manuscripts from ancient times have survived.) Meanwhile Syrian Christians in the East, fascinated by the scientific thought of classical Greece, translated the works of Aristotle, Euclid, Archimedes, Ptolemaeus, Hippocrates and Galen—first into Syriac, then into Arabic. Thus Greek science and medicine, mathematics and philosophy became known, first to the Arabs, then to the Jews and—through Muslim and Jewish scholars in Damascus and Baghdad, Sicily and Spain—to Western Christendom. (Greek learning had also been kept alive in Christian Byzantium, but this only became known in the West after the fall of Constantinople to the Turks in 1453, when medieval civilisation had passed its peak.) We know the *mind* of ancient Greece, Rome and Israel as no other civilisation has ever known the mind of its predecessors. We northern barbarians could start where they left off, once the medieval schools had dinned the basic intellectual tools of grammar, rhetoric and logic into our rather thick skulls.

In *The Lost Tools of Learning*[2] Dorothy L. Sayers points out what a disaster the abandonment of these tools has been for our own society: 'We let our young men and women go out unarmed, in a day when armour was never so necessary. By teaching them all to read, we have left them at the mercy of the printed word. By the invention of the film and the radio'—she wrote before the rise of television—

> we have made certain that no aversion to reading shall secure them from the incessant battery of words, words, words. They do not know what the words mean; they do not know how to ward them off or blunt their edge or fling them back; they are a prey to words in their emotions instead of being masters of them in their intellects. . . . I will say quite firmly that the best grounding for education is the Latin grammar . . . because even a rudimentary

> knowledge of Latin cuts down the labour and pains of learning almost any other subject by at least fifty per cent. It is the key to the vocabulary and structure of all the Romance languages and to the structure of all the Teutonic languages, as well as to the technical vocabulary of all the sciences and the literature of the entire Mediterranean civilisation, together with all its historical documents.

By the twelfth century, the revival of urban life and the rise of cathedral schools and universities was making education available to non-clerics. In *The Discovery of the Individual 1050–1200*,[3] Colin Morris describes how, to the humanists of the twelfth century, the ability to read and write Latin,

> was an essential preliminary to the imaginative exploration of themselves and the universe. What cannot be verbalised can scarcely be thought, and before 1050 the capacity of most writers to express themselves lucidly was poor. . . . The mastery of Latin composition was the most important contribution of humanism to the discovery of the individual. It made possible, for scholarly writers, a naturalness and immediacy of observation, and a subtlety of reflection, which had been impossible in the previous centuries.[4]

Twelfth-century man consciously looked to the past, both Christian and classical, for guidance. The Western belief in the value of the individual is fundamentally Judaeo-Christian. 'A sense of individual identity and value is implicit in belief in a God who has called each man by name, who has sought him out as a shepherd seeks his lost sheep. Self-awareness and a serious concern with inner character is encouraged by the conviction that the believer must lay himself open to God, and be remade by the Holy Spirit.'[5] Among classical writers, the most influential in the twelfth century were probably Cicero, who had already greatly influenced Ambrose in the fourth century and Cassian in the fifth, and the Stoic Seneca, with his concern for self-knowledge and the pursuit of virtue.

The idea of self-knowledge as the way to God, explored by Augustine, was now developed by the Cistercians, especially Bernard of Clairvaux, William of St Thierry and Aelred of Rievaulx. Their interest in psychology led them to study and analyse the 'affections' and the different kinds of love. The older psychology had had a rather simplistic view of the choice between good and evil. A more sophisticated recognition of the multiplicity of the affections and appetites opened the way to a deeper understanding of the individual and a clearer perception of man's place in the universe.[6]

There was a new emphasis on intention and motivation: this was discussed at length by Abelard, for whom sin lay solely in the intention. With the concern for self-knowledge went a new interest in close personal relationships. This period saw the rise of autobiography as a literary form, and of much letter-writing between friends.

The Song of Songs, that very beautiful erotic poem attributed to Solomon, owes its inclusion in the Old Testament canon partly to the ancient tradition of Yahweh as the husband of his people (Hosea 2.16–20). This tradition was understood by early Christians as referring to Christ the Bridegroom and his Bride the Church (Eph. 5.23–32; Rev. 19.7–9; 21.2,9). Already in the third century Origen was interpreting the Song of Songs as an allegory of the spiritual marriage between the individual soul and God. From the twelfth century onward Bernard of Clairvaux's *Sermons on the Canticle* exerted an enormous influence on Christian spirituality. Later the Song of Songs became the foundation of both the medieval Jewish treatise known as the *Zohar* and of the mystical poetry of St John of the Cross.

This was also the age of the troubadours, who sang of the new ideal of courtly love professed by twelfth-century knights—by some as an accepted convention, by others as a genuine personal inspiration. Personal devotion now became seen as the essence of the ideal man–woman relationship, as the Cistercians had made it the focus of the individual's relationship with God. And with the romances of Chrétien de Troyes, the theme of romantic love and of 'marrying for love' enters the European literary tradition.

The thirteenth century was a time of cultural consolidation, of the glories of Gothic architecture—and the aridities of scholasticism. (Thomas Aquinas himself refused to finish his *Summa Theologica*, saying, toward the end of his life, that by comparison with the knowledge of God experienced by him in prayer, all he had written was 'as straw'.) The fourteenth century saw the rise of vernacular literatures—and the apocalyptic horrors of the Black Death, in which a third of the population of Europe perished, with consequent economic and social upheavals. When institutional religion collapses, one's personal relationship with God becomes vital, and the fourteenth century also saw an extraordinary flowering of Christian mysticism, especially in England and the Rhineland. By the fifteenth century, Europe was ready for the new awakening which we call the Renaissance—stimulated by the arrival of Greek scholars fleeing from Byzantium after its fall to the Muslim Turks in 1453.

* * *

But the first time that a whole culture attained the level of personal consciousness was nearly two thousand years earlier. We have noted the link between individuality and literacy, and recognition of personal responsibility in Israel did in fact coincide with their becoming the People of the Book. Literacy was widespread from the eighth century BC onward: there was a reading public for Amos, Hosea, Isaiah and Micah as there had not been for Elijah and Elisha in the ninth century.

In the Exile and Dispersion in the New Testament Gospel is, at last, dimly foreshadowed. It is no accident that so many of our Christmas readings, familiar even to unbelievers through Handel's *Messiah*, come from Second Isaiah. (Old Testament passages seen by Christians as referring to Jesus were not of course so understood when written, nor by Jews to this day: we read the Old Testament in the light of the New; they, in the light of the Talmud.) It is Second Isaiah who most clearly articulates the insights which had to become part of Israel's mental furniture before the events proclaimed in the New Testament Gospel could meaningfully take place among them. These presuppositions are still necessary today if the New Testament Gospel is to be rightly understood.

(1) The first is monotheism and its corollary, creation by that one transcendent God. The gospel of creation must precede the gospel of redemption, or there is nothing to be redeemed. (You do not, for example, 'redeem' the *maya* of the Hindu world-view: you learn to see it to be illusion.)

Those of us old enough to have been brought up within Christendom too lightly take this for granted. The words 'Maker of heaven and earth' slip off the tongue too easily. We don't grasp their staggering import unless or until we have ourselves been forced to transcend our environment and thus to discover (like Israel in the Exile) that our true identity depends, not on our environment or our peer group, but on our God, whom we personally choose to serve regardless of what our neighbours, friends or kinsfolk may be doing. And faith in a transcendent God gives us the courage to make the personal decisions which may separate us from neighbours and kin: transcendence and individuality stand or fall together.

No one in recorded history has expressed the liberating discovery of the one transcendent God more eloquently than Second Isaiah. He significantly addresses Yahweh's proclamation to the Gentile Cyrus, who upon conquering Babylon has told the Jewish exiles that those who wish to do so may return to Jerusalem.

> I am the Lord, and there is no other. There is no god beside me. I girded thee, though thou hast not known me, that they may know from the rising of the sun, and from the west, that there is none beside me. I am the Lord, and there is none else. ... For thus saith the Lord that created the heavens, God himself that formed the earth and made it: ... Look unto me and be ye saved, all the ends of the earth: for I am God, and there is no other. (Isaiah 45.5–6, 18, 22)

'I am God, *and there is no other.*' This is very different from the Deuteronomic proclamation (5.6–7) to the closed community of Israel in their Promised Land: 'I am the Lord *thy* God, which brought thee out of the land of Egypt, from the house of bondage. *Thou* shalt have none other gods before me.' And the implications are very different. Deuteronomy speaks to those still being formed in community; Isaiah sounds a clarion call to mission in the Dispersion. To the extent that Christians really are monotheists with no other gods, we recognise Isaiah's call as addressed to us. Those who see Christianity as merely the tribal religion of the West see no need for mission and may even regard it as inappropriate.

(2) The second presupposition of the New Testament Gospel is the individuality which makes it possible for the disciples to 'leave all' and follow Jesus (Luke 14.25–33; Matt. 10.34–39).

When community crumbles, personal responsibility becomes vital. In the Exile the earlier Hebrew concern for persons chiefly as members of a family, clan, tribe, nation, gives way to an increasing recognition of individuality in all people, not just in charismatic heroes. Jeremiah sees that exile and dispersion call for a new covenant in which each individual, no longer dependent on communal oral tradition *about* God, has direct personal knowledge *of* him. This is announced as the culmination of a passage (31.29–34) about the emergence of personal responsibility. The Deuteronomist (24.16) has already proclaimed the new ethic: 'The fathers shall not be put to death for the children, nor shall children be put to death for the fathers; every man shall be put to death for his *own* sin.' Ezekiel, writing in the Exile, expounds this principle at great length (ch. 18 and 33.10–20).

It is of vital importance in modern societies. A tribal ethic limits moral obligations to kinsmen; strangers are fair game. In *The African Predicament*[7] Stanlisav Andreski describes the problems this raises as tribal people move into great cities where most encounters are with non-kinsmen and where the concept of neighbour (*who*ever he is) has not replaced that of kinsman (*where*ver he is) as the controlling factor in ethics). All ethnic, religious or other group prejudice is a manifestation of the tribal ethic. *Human* rights are meaningless unless each individual is seen as a person in his or her own right, regardless of any group affiliation. But very many shrink from the loneliness, and the responsibilities, of being a person. Growth in consciousness is almost always resisted at first.

The New Testament word for 'church', *ekklesia*, means literally 'called out', and those who become Christians as adults by their own personal decision are just that. Even today it can be a costly calling, setting one at odds with kith and kin and peer group (Matthew 10.35–37). A Jew or a Hindu who is baptised may be read out of the family and henceforth regarded as dead. In some countries a Muslim who is baptised risks actual death, for some Muslim extremists regard apostasy from Islam as a capital offence. Abraham was called to 'go out', and in the New Testament he is seen as the type of man of faith in every generation (Romans 4; Galatians 3.6–9; Hebrews 11.8–19).

(3) The third presupposition of the New Testament (as of the Old) is a sense of history. Human perception of time varies greatly, both in different cultures and at different stages of our own individual growth.[8] Probably two-thirds of mankind live in a non-historical dimension of time. Asked what was the greatest obstacle today to the ordinary man's acceptance of the Christian faith, C. S. Lewis once replied 'He doesn't believe in history'. He believes, Lewis said, in an enormous tract of time, very real ('the present'), in which he lives. Behind this is another tract with some rather shadowy reality ('when Dad was a boy'); behind that, another tract of time with very little reality at all ('the old days'). Behind that are only 'knights in armour, monks in monasteries, Henry VIII and all his wives, with Julius Caesar romping about in the middle—and that's Hans Andersen!'[9]

History as Christians understand it begins with the Hebrew prophets, though the prophets would not have understood historical time quite as modern Europeans do, for biblical Hebrew has no past, present or future tenses. The Hebrew perfect and imperfect represent (respectively) completed and incompleted action—which may be located (according to our Indo-European reckoning) in the past, the present or the future. (Such Semitic thinking lies, for example, behind the apocalyptic visions in the Book of Revelation, which when written down in Greek—or in English—speak of future events as if they had already taken place: what we call a *fait accompli*.) But the ancient Hebrews did understand history as time in which significant events really happen and should be remembered; time with a purpose, going from somewhere to somewhere; time in which God acts to change things and in which men (no longer slaves to fate or any other kind of determinism, economic or technological) can act to change things. History so understood is the context which gives meaning to the present and motivation to the future.

This is not the same as the modern notion of 'objective' or 'scientific' history concerning 'what really happened', with its passion for factual accuracy and critical investigation of sources. We cannot know what really happened, for even if we had been there at the time, what we would have seen would (like any observation) have depended partly on what we expected to see: the discrepancies between different eyewitness accounts of the same event are notorious. All historical writing involves selection and interpretation of data on the basis of somebody's judgement as to what is significant. But meaning only emerges in retrospect. Since we are still in the middle of the story, every historian must make an act of faith concerning the end, which determines the meaning of all that goes before. *Any* 'fact of history' is an interpretation of evidence according to some presuppositions. Strictly speaking, therefore, there is no such thing as 'objective history', just as modern physicists acknowledge that in the material world there is no such thing as an 'objective fact' independent of the perception of the observer: there are only probabilities.

The Bible interprets the whole of human history as a saga beginning with creation and ending with the gathering of all nations and the fulfilment of God's purpose for all mankind and for all creation. Until fairly recent times, this biblical world-view was the context within which world history was taught in the West.

Lesslie Newbigin, who has spent much of his life in India, has described[10] the gulf that exists between the children of Abraham and the 'timeless East', and how *secular* Western influence confronts India and the East with the claims of Christ. The modern scientific/technological world civilisation could have arisen only in a part of the world dominated by biblical beliefs about the created world and man's place in it. ('It could not occur in Europe until the grip of the Aristotelian world-view upon the European mind was broken. It is difficult to believe that it could have occurred at all within the world-views of the dominant Asian religions.'[11]) It includes as its driving force the conviction that human life can and should be *changed*. 'This belief has become so familiar to us in the West that we forget that it runs counter to the religious faith of at least half the human race. Most ancient religions interpret the movement of events in terms of recurrent cycles. The idea of linear movement in a single direction is incompatible with their deepest convictions.'[12] (They have not yet made their Exodus and pilgrimage to Mount Sinai.) Yet India's five-year plans did not anticipate a return to the starting-point: the old cyclic Hindu calendar will no longer do. More and more of the world is adopting the time-reckoning that moves in a single irreversible line from the birth of Christ, though some prefer to write dates BCE (Before Common Era) and CE (Common Era) rather than BC and AD.

Many peoples (Newbigin observes) have had no history because they did not believe anything significant ever really happened. Others have had local tribal histories.

Now all are being drawn into a single world history whose driving force is the idea (Christian or Marxist) of a new order in the future. People everywhere now have messianic expectations. The issues are posed from within the Christian tradition even by those who reject the Christian faith: welfare states and the concept of human rights are based on a valuation of the individual (even the apparently useless individual) which is rooted in the Gospel and which transcends membership of any tribe, race, religion or culture.

(4) The fourth presupposition of the New Testament Gospel which is first articulated in the Exile is a shift in the traditional attitude to suffering. It is the new insistence on individual responsibility before God which raises the problem of Job. In the old communal ethic all, whether personally innocent or guilty, expect to suffer when any member of the community has sinned, as when the entire household of Achan are put to death for his trespass (Joshua 7). But if the individual is to be recompensed solely for his own actions, how is it that a good man suffers? In the end Job is reduced to silence before the mystery of God.

The answer to Job cannot be fully expounded until after the crucifixion and resurrection of God himself in Christ. But the clue is offered in the Servant Songs, which link the redemptive use of innocent suffering with Israel's mission to the nations (Isaiah 53 with 49.6).

The traditional Old Testament view regards suffering as a sign of God's displeasure. This is the view of Job's friends and of the conventional wisdom: 'never have I seen the righteous forsaken, nor his seed begging their bread' (Psalm 37.25). It is a view expressly repudiated by Jesus (Luke 13.1–5) but it dies hard.

All religions have something to say about suffering. Hinduism teaches that suffering in this life results from wrong-doing in a previous life. Islam, which sees the truth of Muhammad's teaching as vindicated by his victory over his adversaries—and by Islam's triumph over rival faiths—does not find it easy to cope with failure or suffering other than by patient submission to the will of God (Islam means 'submission').[13] Buddhism assumes suffering to be self-evidently the worst evil: its Four Noble Truths are the fact of suffering, the cause of suffering (desire), the cessation of suffering (renunciation of desire) and the Eightfold Path of discipline by which one may *escape from* suffering. The Christian gospel shows us what to *do with* our suffering. Most contemporary social and political thinking takes for granted something not unlike the Buddhist attitude. The Christian view is set forth in 1 Peter 2.19–25, which quotes Isaiah 53 with explicit reference to Jesus. St Paul's epistles make clear that faithful witnesses to Christ must expect to share in his sufferings.

* * *

The practical problem for the Hebrew exiles is how, against the pressures of an alien culture, to maintain their identity as the people of God and to form each new generation. Unlike the refugees who came out of Egypt with Moses, these exiles are neither slaves nor a mixed multitude. They are the articulate upper and middle classes of a structured society (2 Kings 24.12–16)—the literate priests and scribes and court officials, the nobility, the skilled craftsmen. (The 'poorer sort of people of the land' have been left behind, still rooted in the soil.)

The exiles' solution to their problem leads to Israel's becoming the People of the Book, with what must eventually have been the highest literacy rate in the ancient world.[14] (By our Lord's time a Jewish boy was expected by the age of twelve to be able to stand up in the synagogue and read from the scriptures.) Oral traditions were collected and written down, and existing records edited. Then they had to be copied, preserved, and handed down. To this day, the central cult object in any synagogue is the Torah scroll.

Most recorded history is written by conquerors and represents the official view of an Establishment. But in the Exile an articulate élite experienced subjection to an alien power. Much of the Old Testament therefore represents an underdog's-eye-view of history such as is rarely preserved in writing. The New Testament is the work of a persecuted minority. Both convey the insights of outsiders who see through official pretensions and accepted conventions to what God is saying and doing.

Jewish awareness of the need diligently to teach their traditions to each succeeding generation is seen especially in Exodus 12.24–27 and chapter 13, Deuteronomy 4.1–9; 6.6–9, 20–24; 11.18–20, and Psalm 78.1–8. God's revelation consists of events plus their interpretation and is not thought self-evident to the uninstructed.

The exiles evolve a new kind of worship. The liturgical drama of the temple with its daily sacrifices is a thing of the past, to be remembered and mediated upon. Though the temple is eventually rebuilt and its sacrificial system restored by those who return to Jerusalem with Ezra and Nehemiah, these exiles also bring back with them the new type of worship (Nehemiah 8). There were synagogues in Jerusalem in the time of Jesus, alongside the temple. The local gathering of the synagogue (which must have started as a sort of 'house church') is an occasion for reading aloud and expounding the writings which were coming to be regarded as scripture, for singing psalms and for blessing God in prayer. It is literate worship, the ancestor alike of the monastic daily offices and of the Protestant type of worship derived from them, centred around the Word of God.

The sabbath rest, which also seems to have become institutionalised in the Exile, not only facilitates such a weekly 'return to the roots' of communal identity. It has a cosmic significance as a return to Paradise, celebrating the joy of God's creation before any human intervention (which is why one abstains from work) and an anticipation of the messianic age when all will have been restored. The sabbath has been for Jews of the Dispersion a sort of portable homeland. Without the temple, they are still able to live within the drama of their liturgical year.

In home and synagogue, this is the formation of the dispersed, and it is a literate formation. (Much the same formative function has been served over wide areas in modern times by the Christian mission school.) A new kind of functionary emerges, the rabbi or teacher, and a tradition of literate scholarship, with a body of both oral and written commentary. The command and warning contained in Deuteronomy 6.4–15, originally uttered in a Canaanite context, become even more urgent in the Dispersion:

> Hear, O Israel: the Lord our God is one Lord; and you shall love the Lord your God with all your heart, and with all your soul, and with all your might. And these words which I command you this day shall be upon your heart; and you shall teach them diligently to your children, and shall talk of them when you sit in your house, and when you walk by the way, and when you lie down, and when you rise. ... Take heed lest you forget the Lord, who brought you out of the land of Egypt, out of the house of bondage. You shall fear the Lord your God; you shall serve him, and swear by his name. You shall not go after other gods, of the gods of the peoples who are round about you; for the Lord your God in the midst of you is a jealous God; lest the anger of the Lord your God be kindled against you, and he destroy you from off the face of the earth.

The first part of this passage, as the *Shema*, remains basic to Jewish piety to this day. It is cited by Jesus (Mark 12.29–30) as 'the first and great commandment'.

The chance for some of the exiles to return to Jerusalem comes with the fall of Babylon to Cyrus the Persian. Only a minority choose to do so. The majority have settled down very comfortably in Babylon.[15] But it is those who do return who are the pioneers of Judaism as we have come to know it. It is now that the Pentateuch and the Book of Joshua reach their final form, edited by priestly scribes (of whom Ezra is the archetype) with an overwhelming concern for the temple and its worship. As the covenant at Shechem (Joshua 24) had incorporated into the Exodus faith those who had not shared the Exodus experience, so now the minority who return to Jerusalem under Nehemiah impose their faith and practice on those who have not experienced the Exile (Nehemiah 8–13)—as well as on those who, having settled down in Babylon, no longer regard it as exile.

The prophet Zechariah has misgivings about the plan to rebuild the city walls: 'Jerusalem shall be inhabited as towns *without* walls. . . . For I will be unto her a wall of fire round about' (2.4–5 AV). Zechariah foresees the fulfilment of Israel's mission to the nations through the attractiveness of her way of life: men of every nation will say 'We will go with you, for we have heard that God is with you' (8.23 AV). It will be among Gentiles who have done just that—'God-fearers' attracted to the synagogue by the Jewish way of life—that the Christian Gospel will first spread.

But the temptation to regress proves too strong, and the zeal of Ezra and Nehemiah rebuilds walls not only of stone but of the Law, in order to keep the closed community closed. The universalism of Second Isaiah is almost forgotten. Yet in the providence of God the exclusiveness of post-exilic Judaism enables the people of God to maintain their identity through all attempts to assimilate them into the cosmopolitan Hellenistic culture which was the 'Western civilisation' of the day. Many succumb to that culture's worldly attractions (1 Maccabees 1.11–15, 2 Maccabees 4.7–15); the Book of Ecclesiasticus was most likely written to strengthen the resistance of the faithful. The anger of the Greek king Antiochus Epiphanes at the refusal of this obstinate minority of his subjects to conform produces the earliest known religious martyrs (2 Maccabees 6, 7).

* * *

In post-exilic Judaism the word *Torah*, which strictly speaking refers to the Pentateuch, is used of the whole way of life centred on devotion to the will of God and the hallowing of his Name. The Septuagint Greek version of the Old Testament translates *Torah* as *nomos*, 'law', but Torah is by no means the dry legalism sometimes supposed. Perhaps the finest biblical expression is Psalm 119, exuberant with the disciple's joy in loving obedience:

> Oh how I love thy law!
> It is my meditation all the day long.   (Psalm 119.97)

In Christian tradition the daily recitation of this psalm forms the core of the monastic 'lesser offices' of Prime, Terce, Sext and None.

By our Lord's time, the custodians of Torah were the Pharisees, who had risen to prominence during the previous century and a half at a time when Judaism and Jewish society were undergoing profound changes in response to the challenge of Hellenism. The Pentateuch envisages a predominantly agricultural peasant society. But as Jews moved into the towns and cities of the Hellenistic world they faced problems undreamt of in the written Law (the only Law the conservative Sadducees recognised) and experienced the loneliness of the individual in a cosmopolitan society. A body of unwritten 'oral Law' evolved (said, like the written Law, to have been revealed to Moses on Sinai) which reinterpreted the written Law to meet the needs of an increasingly urbanised society of merchants, artisans, shopkeepers and intellectuals. To this society (according to Ellis Rivkin, a distinguished American rabbi who reckons himself a latter-day Pharisee) the Pharisees proclaimed that '(1) God the just and caring Father so loved each and every individual that (2) he revealed to Israel his twofold Law—Written and Oral—which, when *internalised* and faithfully obeyed, (3) promises to the Law-abiding individual eternal life for his soul and resurrection for his body. Internalisation of the divine will as the ultimate, the most certain, and the only enduring reality—this was the grand achievement of the Scribes-Pharisees.'[16]

Belief in the resurrection of the body (a very different matter from the pagan belief in the natural immortality of the soul) coincides with the rise of individuality. Most Old Testament references to life after death concern *she'ōl*, which (like the pagan underworld) is a place where disembodied spirits live a shadowy half-existence in alienation from God. So long as one's consciousness is centred in the group ('I belong; therefore I am') it is enough that one should live on in one's descendants and in the life of the tribe or clan. But with the rise of personal consciousness and of personal relationships which are not mere roles in the communal drama, personal survival becomes important. The only clear Old Testament references to resurrection are very late: Isaiah 26.19 is part of an apocalyptic passage several centuries later than the historical Isaiah; Daniel 12.2 dates from the time of the Maccabaean martyrs, 168–165 BC. Because the Pentateuch contains no mention of resurrection, the Sadducees rejected that belief, along with everything else in the oral Law.

The spirituality of this level of consciousness—of the individual who must be able to move about freely in a cosmopolitan world—is that of a personal discipleship which, through self-discipline, pursues moral perfection according to an interiorised ideal. (It corresponds, more or less, to the 'Illuminative Way' of traditional Christian spirituality.)

Such a quest was not of course peculiar to Jews. There were pagan philosopher-sages and their disciples in the Greco-Roman world—Socrates, Plato, the Stoics and others. But the internalised standard which they taught was an option only for the sophisticated few. For the masses, steeped in polytheism, there could be no single internalised standard, for they did not have a single God. 'To internalise the pantheon of the Greeks and Romans was to internalise chaos, conflict, and discord. It was to internalise congeries of mutually exclusive demands, prohibitions, and ego ideals. It simply made a one-to-One relationship impossible, for there was no One.'[17]

Pagan Greek thought never came to terms with the philosophical problem of the One, the Singular. Until the rise of Christianity brought Hebrew insistence on one God face to face with Greek philosophy, the Greeks dismissed the singular as essentially unknowable. Aristotle thought the individual knowable only as a particular instance of a universal rule. But as J. V. Langmead Casserley points out in *The Christian in Philosophy*,[18] there is a profound distinction between the particular and the singular:

> The 'particular' is the individual as seen by the man who is looking for the universal, and who will feel baffled intellectually until he finds it; the 'singular' is the individual seen from the point of view of the man who is out to capture and enjoy the full flavour of its individuality. ... The particular is the individual seen through the eye of the empirical scientist, whereas the singular is the individual seen from the historian's point of view.

—a point of view shared with the dramatist, the metaphysician, the theologian, the religious devotee and the man in the street.

The Greeks understood only two kinds of inference, deduction from universals and induction from particulars, but not the third kind, which leads to conclusions about singulars (e.g. 'the prisoner is innocent'). But this is just what Christian theology is concerned with: 'it is the study of the singular, indeed the Absolute Singular, God, who has disclosed his nature to us in the singular series of events which provide the subject matter of the Bible'. And it is this third kind of inference which makes possible both the pursuit of history as a serious science and also the understanding of human beings in terms of personality—developments which Casserley calls 'the two most profound and revealing events in the intellectual history of the Christian era'. Both were made possible by theology's vindication of the claims of the singular.

It was the Cappadocian Fathers[19] in the fourth century who took the decisive step. In their wrestling with the biblical account of the self-manifestation of God, they needed to express both the essential unity of the Godhead and also its revealed diversity. They made what was to prove an epoch-making distinction between two Greek terms, *ousia* and *hypostasis*, hitherto used almost interchangeably:

> Henceforward *ousia* was to signify the unity of the Godhead, the common essence which made the persons one, while *hypostasis* was to be employed to underline the distinctions between them, to denote those characteristics peculiar to each which rendered it right and necessary for us in some sense to separate the inseparable in our thought and devotion. In other words, *hypostasis* was re-defined so as to represent the singular become at last a proper subject of knowledge.

And when Latin theologians, seeking an equivalent to *hypostasis*, chose the legal and dramatic term *persona*, the idea of personality was born—personality in God first and then, in the image of God, in man.

The Pharisees internalised the personal relationship of the individual with the one true God and Rivkin sees this Pharisaic revolution as underlying all three of the great monotheistic religions. With the final destruction of the temple in AD 70 and the consequent disappearance of both the Zealots and the priestly Sadducees, the heirs of the Pharisees became the acknowledged leaders of rabbinic Judaism. Henceforth the Pentateuch, the prophets, and the other scriptural writings were to be understood by Jews only through the interpretation of the oral Law (the Mishnah), which reached its final written form *ca* AD 200. The Mishnah and the seemingly endless commentaries on it (the Gemara) evolved during the first six centuries of the Christian era (and partly in response to the Christian challenge) into that vast encyclopaedia of rabbinic wisdom which is the Talmud. Jesus and his disciples were brought up in the Pharisaic tradition. So was Saul of Tarsus, who substituted the risen Christ for the twofold Law as the ultimate Reality to be internalised. Six centuries later Islam substituted the will of God as revealed to Muhammad in the Qur'an for the twofold Law as that which the true Muslim is to internalise.

* * *

The temptation to regress, or to cling to reassuring structures and certainties in the face of a challenge to move on, is perennial. Jeremiah warned (ch. 7) against reliance on the first temple. Six centuries later a Greek-speaking Jew named Stephen gave his life in a vain attempt to wean the Jerusalem Establishment from their blind reliance on the second temple.

Between the stoning of Stephen and the destruction of the temple in AD 70 the whole of the New Testament (as I believe) took shape[20] and church and synagogue gradually drew apart as the dialogue between them sharpened. Nowhere was this dialogue sharper than in Caesarea, the great seaport built by Herod the Great and adopted by the Romans as their capital, where tension between Jew and Gentile always ran high. After Jerusalem itself, Caesarea was the most important centre of Palestinian Christianity, with the first Christian school of higher biblical studies and a library which continued to develop down to the time of Origen, Eusebius and Jerome. The Gospel according to Matthew was very likely produced here,[21] in and for a community concerned to set out its own position (over against both Pharisaic and Sadducean Judaism) regarding scripture, the Law, the temple and its sacrifices, the sabbath, marriage and divorce, prayer, fasting, food laws. It reflects what is known of the situation in Palestine *ca* AD 50–64; like the Epistle to the Hebrews, it assumes that the Levitical system is still operating and offers a Christian alternative. Luke, too, was probably based in Caesarea during Paul's two years' detention there AD 57–59.

It was in Caesarea that in AD 66 the First Revolt began, spreading quickly throughout the country. In 68 the Christian community in Jerusalem fled across the Jordan to Pella. The following year Rabbi Yohanan ben Zakkai, who had escaped from the siege of Jerusalem, was allowed by

Vespasian to go to a refugee camp at Yavneh (Jamnia), south of Jaffa. In 70 Jerusalem fell, the temple was burnt and the city levelled.

For the second time in Jewish history, seemingly, the bottom had dropped out of their universe. But this time they had the Law, both oral and written, and already in Yavneh a group of scholars were meeting daily with Yohanan ben Zakkai to study Torah and to determine how its observance could best be safeguarded. Gradually they codified the *halakhah* (oral law) and the canon of the Hebrew Bible. Decisions were made about the calendar, festivals and holy days; the Passover *haggadah* took much its present form, without the sacrifice of the paschal lamb. This court of Law at Yavneh became a great centre of Jewish scholarship, replacing the Sanhedrin of Jerusalem, which was no more.

Thus was born rabbinic Judaism, which (freed from dependence on the temple and its sacrificial system) turned inward, away from wars and politics and public life. Content now to live above history and its problems, the rabbis focussed instead on practical wisdom and the meaning of ordinary daily life: how does one sanctify God's Name here and now? Henceforth the most important activity of Jewish life would be study.

'Rabbinic Judaism,' says the Jewish historian Jacob Neusner,[22] 'came, in time, to set itself up as the alternative to all forms of messianic Judaism—whether in the form of Christianity or militaristic zealotry and nationalism—which claimed to know the secret of history, the time of salvation, and the way to redemption.' The closed community, seeking the sanctification of one people set apart to be holy, seemed to have forgotten the universalism of Second Isaiah and the mission to the Gentiles.

In AD 131 Hadrian, like Antiochus Epiphanes before him, tried to force the Jews to assimilate. He founded a Roman colony at Jerusalem, with a temple to Jupiter on the site of the Jewish temple and a shrine to Venus on the Christian Calvary.[23] The Second Revolt broke out in 132.

In 135 the Jews were expelled from Jerusalem, Judaea was laid waste and its name changed to Palestine. Half a million Jews perished. Most of the rest, including the scholars from Yavneh, moved to the Galilee. It was there that the Palestinian Talmud took shape. In the Byzantine period, the centre of Jewish scholarship moved to Bablyonia. Gradually the Talmud displaced scripture as the final authority in Judaism, written Torah being relegated to elementary instruction.

By 150 the Jewish Christian community were re-established in Jerusalem, together with growing numbers of Greek Christians, and pilgrims. Despite the increasing domination of Byzantine Greeks, a Semitic church with its own bishop survived in Jerusalem until the beginning of the fifth century.

When the Arab conquest of 638 brought Muslim rule, most Palestinians were at least partly of Jewish descent. Modern Palestinians are descended from everyone who has ever lived in the land: from the Canaanites, who were there before Abraham; from the Philistines, from whom Palestine takes its name; from the Arabs, most of whom came from 638 onward; but also from the Jews who never left. Every conqueror—Assyrian, Babylonian, Persian, Greek, Roman, Arab, Turk—brought its own ruling class and military establishment, but the peasant majority were left largely undisturbed—to till the soil and pay the taxes.

In 638, despite Byzantine efforts to stamp out Judaism, perhaps twenty-five per cent of Palestinians were still of Jewish religion, though many Jews had gone to join the Dispersion in Babylonia or elsewhere. (The size of the synagogues built in the Byzantine period—e.g. at Bet Alpha, Hammat-Tiberias, Chorazin, Capernaum, Baram and Hammat-Gadar in the Galilee, at Eshtemoa and Suseya in the Judaean hills near Hebron, at En-Gedi by the Dead Sea—testifies to the size and prosperity of the Jewish communities they served.) Most of the rest had by now become Christian. Because Palestinians resented being dominated by Byzantine Greeks, many welcomed the Arabs as liberators. And because of the state of both Christianity and Judaism in the land at that time, many willingly accepted the Muslim claim that Islam was not a new religion but simply a call to return to their own primitive faith—rather like the Protestant Reformation in Europe. But many others remained Christian (or Jewish), taxed but tolerated as monotheistic People of the Book. In the time of the Crusades, the behaviour of the Crusaders (who slaughtered Eastern Christians as well as Muslims and Jews) so appalled the Christians of the land that the majority now embraced Islam. But a minority of Palestinians remain Christian to this day.

There were Arabs among the 'devout Jews of every nation' living in Jerusalem on the Day of Pentecost (Acts 2.5–11). Ramleh, near Lydda, was founded by Muslim Arabs in the eighth century as their capital; and Ramallah, on the West Bank, by a Christian tribe that moved there from Arabia in the sixteenth century. But though all Palestinians are now 'Arabs' in language and culture, they are only partly of Arab descent. Genetically speaking, the children of Abraham, Isaac and Jacob must be at least as well represented on the West Bank as in Tel Aviv.

Judaism's turning inward after AD 70 represents a defensive regression to tribal consciousness, a regression forced upon them by the disaster precipitated by Zealot fanaticism. Modern Zionism, despite its terrible cost to another people, is for most Jews a creative regression to a rootedness in the land which has always been a part of Jewish identity. But this time the regression has been forced upon them by the way we Gentiles have behaved toward our Lord's own people among us in Christendom.

The slanderous and abhorrent ideology which has led to persecution, pogroms, and the final horror of the Holocaust has theological roots in a cruel misinterpretation of certain passages in the gospels. Matthew 27.26 ('His blood be upon us and our children') may well have been uttered in the heat of the moment by a mob stirred up by followers of Barabbas and by agitators planted by the Sanhedrin, but anti-semitic polemic has used this as an excuse for stereotyping Jewish people throughout history as 'Christ-killers'.

In the Fourth Gospel the Greek *Ioudaioi* is usually translated simply 'the Jews', which has made it easy for this Gospel to be seen as 'anti-semitic'. But of course Jesus himself and all his disciples were Jews, as were all the first Christians until the baptism of Cornelius (Acts 10), and the Galilean Jews clearly welcomed Jesus. Where the evangelist (himself a Jew) speaks of those who opposed Jesus and plotted his death, *Ioudaioi* refers to the Judaean Jews of the Jerusalem Establishment, to whom Jesus was indeed a threat—the Jewish authorities. But even in Jerusalem 'the common people heard him gladly' (Mark 12.37). This profoundest of all Christian theological documents was probably first produced for the Greek-speaking Jewish Christians of Jerusalem before being edited for the Gentile mission in Ephesus.[24] It needs to be rescued from the anti-semitic misuse that has sometimes been made of it.

Anti-semitism, like apartheid (which has also been given theological justification, by generations of Afrikaner Christians) is indeed an evil that must be totally rejected.[25] But discrediting the ideology does not remove the gut fear and hatred experienced by the insecure when faced with people who are 'different'. The real problem—that which evokes such justifying ideologies—is that, despite our Christian profession, in practice we, too, have failed to grow up from a culturally homogeneous tribal community into a *koinonia* capable of tolerating internal diversity.

The perennial human craving for a scapegoat to blame for all one's misfortunes and onto whom to project one's own unacknowledged 'shadow' is the real root of all forms of racism and ethnic hatred. And since the one indispensable qualification of scapegoats is that they must be identifiable, Jewish persistence in maintaining the separateness of *their* community casts them, unavoidably, in the role of potential scapegoat. It is the dark shadow of their chosenness.

And the ghetto, which before its medieval legal enforcement was a social institution born of Jewish solidarity and Gentile aversion, has over the centuries become a mentality. Your own identity comes to depend on the hostility of your neighbours; that there could ever be friends on the other side of the fence is literally unthinkable. This is no small part of the dilemma of the modern State of Israel in its dealings with its neighbours.

It is a peculiarly tragic irony that Palestinian Muslims and Christians, who lived quite happily with Palestinian Jews until Zionist immigrants began to take over, should suffer for our European sins. What to the immigrants was an 'ingathering of exiles' coming home was experienced by the Palestinians as a foreign invasion, which was understandably resisted, with increasing violence on both sides. The 1948 war left the State of Israel established on two-thirds of the land; the rest was occupied in 1967. For Christian Arabs (and ten per cent of all Arabs are Christian) the dispossession is spiritual as well as geographical, for it has become incredibly difficult for them to use the Old Testament. And Western Christian behaviour, from the fourth century (when we were first in a position of power) to the present, must constitute an almost insuperable barrier to Jewish acceptance of Jesus. We Western Christians have much to answer for at the Day of Judgement.

Meanwhile we would do well to rediscover our own Jewish roots, for whenever this heritage is forgotten, the danger of Christianity's turning into either a gnostic mystery religion or a political ideology is never far away. Jesus and the apostles were observant Jews for whom 'the scriptures' were what we call the Old Testament, and apart from Luke/Acts the whole of the New Testament was also written by Jews. The Good News presupposes the Jewish experience of God's self-revelation; its extension to non-Jews was an unexpected and traumatic experience for the early church (Acts 10; 11; 13.13–49). St Paul's agonising in Romans 9–11 makes clear that he had 'turned to the Gentiles' (Acts 13.46), not as abandoning Israel, but in order that through the conversion of the Gentiles Israel herself may be saved, for she cannot come to the fulfilment of God's purpose for her until she can countenance the inclusion of the *goyim*—until the exclusive community becomes the inclusive koinonia of the People of God. In St Paul's vision, the Church is meant to be the *enlarged* Israel, not (as was said later in anti-semitic polemic) a substitute for it.

Schism between synagogue and church only became final with the Second Revolt of 132–135, in which Christian Jews refused to participate.[26] Since then we have, tragically, gone our separate ways. Judaism did not end with the Old Testament, and there is much that we could learn today from the wisdom of the rabbis, and from the on-going witness of God's ancient people to the revelation given to them by God for all humanity.

* * *

The Pharisees have had a bad press. Earnest, pious middle-class lay theologians, they were a protest movement against the corrupt, worldly (and aristocratic) Sadducees of the priestly Establishment in Jerusalem. The whole point of Jesus's denunciation of them is that fundamentally they were a Good Thing, representing the best in Israel—yet even *that* great tradition had its dark shadow of self-righteousness and hypocrisy and was unable, ultimately, to make men whole.

The Pharisees were the bearers in their day of the 'Puritan ethic' to which, despite all, the world owes more than it mostly cares, just now, to admit. For there can be no true freedom without previous subjection to law: without that formative discipline, there is only unrecognised slavery to impulse within and environmental pressure without. Those of us fortunate enough to have had in our upbringing some measure of the Puritan ethic and its (yes, middle-class) disciplines ought to thank God daily for it, even if we have subsequently had to break out of its rigidities in order to keep on growing.

II

The Stone that the Builders Rejected

Because each one of us must climb the ladder of psychic evolution for himself, there are always people at various stages, and only a minority of those living at any given time have become sufficiently conscious to cope with individuality. There is always tension between the communal values of the majority and those which foster individuality in cosmopolitan societies. The two kinds of values are complementary: both are needed if we are to be fully human; it ought not to be an either/or. But in the past two or three centuries the tension between the communal and individual levels of consciousness has become sharply polarised. It is a factor in most of our political and social divisions and is central in the struggle for human rights.

There are two main reasons for this increased polarisation. The first concerns the *pace* of change. We have noted the 'splitting' which must take place within each one of us in order to form a conscious ego. In traditional communities it is socially acceptable and even patriotic to project our unacceptable shadow onto tacitly recognised scapegoats (enemies, aliens, criminals). But when the dominant culture proclaims the ideal of brotherly love for *all*, there are no more socially approved scapegoats, so the repressed shadow can no longer be openly projected. The growth of rational consciousness thus involves a corresponding accumulation of irrationality in the collective unconscious.

There is an African proverb which warns you not to travel further by day than your soul can catch up by night. Since about the time of Descartes the differentiation of consciousness in the West has gone too fast in the daylight of reason for the majority to keep up. We have exceeded the psychic speed limit, and the European psyche has been split. Rationality has turned into an arid and brittle rational*ism*, cut off from its unconscious roots. And the brighter the light, the darker the shadow: the rationalist Enlightenment evoked the Romantic glorification of the dark, irrational 'feeling' side of human experience; the French Revolution had no sooner enthroned the goddess of Reason in the place of God than it lapsed into the irrationalities of the Terror.

The pioneers break through into the exhilarating new dimension of individuality, but (being only human) too often fall into selfish individual*ism* instead of using their enhanced abilities for the common good. The self-centredness of the infant layer of their personalities overpowers the sense of communal responsibility evolved in the childhood/tribal layer.

Meanwhile those unable or unwilling to adapt, regress—for in times of turbulent change we cannot stand still. Some retreat into the tribalism of mutually hostile ethnic or other solidarities. Others are drawn into one of the resurgent fundamentalisms of our day: in times of insecurity, the offer of certainty becomes powerfully attractive.

Islamic fundamentalism is a deliberate rejection of Western civilisation and its values. Writing in 1986 about the Iranian revolution led by the Ayatollah Khomeini, Lesslie Newbigin asked 'why do the present leaders of that country denounce America and Russian equally as agents of Satan? Because they have seen the fabric of their own society, its family life, its sexual ethics, and its ideas of what human life is for, disintegrating under the influence of ideas coming through both these channels that stem from the European Enlightenment.'[1] The Enlightenment itself, and the secularisation which it brought, came about in no small measure in revulsion from the religious wars of seventeenth-century Europe. Today we can perceive the ambiguity of both rationalism and religious fervour.

The other main reason for this increased polarisation has

to do with the question of *size*, which is a far more potent factor in human affairs than is usually recognised. Social and political ideals such as participatory democracy, which work well in small city-states like those of ancient Greece, notoriously become compromised in empires like that of ancient Rome—and in large modern bureaucratic states. Aristotle said a country is too big if you can't see across it. 'How can masses of this kind conceivably be organised as a community?' asks Jacques Ellul concerning the post-Constantinian church.² This is the underlying fallacy of Marxism. 'Good human relations, in my experience,' said the late E. F. (*Small is Beautiful*) Schumacher, 'are extremely difficult, if not impossible, to attain in large units, whether these are schools, universities, offices, or factories. Participation, so rightly demanded in industry and elsewhere, cannot become a reality when units are so large and complex that people cannot know each other as people and the minds of ordinary men and women cannot encompass the meaning and ramifications of the whole.'³

Leopold Kohr, a political philosopher whose seminal book *The Breakdown of Nations*⁴ greatly influenced Schumacher, goes even further: 'wherever something is wrong, something is too big'. Behind all forms of social misery Kohr sees one cause: *bigness*. And this is no isolated phenomenon, but the operation of what seems to be a fundamental principle throughout creation: that all things have their proper size, which cannot with impunity be exceeded.

> If the stars in the sky or the atoms of uranium disintegrate in spontaneous explosion, it is not because their substance has lost its balance. It is because matter has attempted to expand beyond the impassable barriers set to every accumulation. Their mass has become too big. If the human body becomes diseased, it is, as in cancer, because a cell, or a group of cells, has begun to outgrow its allotted narrow limits. And if the body of a people becomes diseased with the fever of aggression, brutality, collectivism, or massive idiocy, it is not because it has fallen victim to bad leadership or mental derangement. It is because human beings, so

charming as individuals or in small aggregations, have been welded into overconcentrated social units such as mobs, unions, cartels, or great powers.⁵

Kohr is particularly critical of large nation-states which are not really nations at all, but which incorporate (almost always against their will) a variety of ethnic and cultural minorities who would greatly prefer self-determination in their own small independent states. The restlessness of the constituent republics of the Soviet Union surfaced the moment the iron hand of central control began to loosen; in the last months of 1991 the USSR itself ceased to exist. Yugoslavia has been torn apart by the immemorial ethnic hatreds and fears of the Balkans. Separatist movements among ethnic minorities increasingly challenge the integrity of nation states in many parts of the world.

And yet—in a world made up entirely of mini-states, *who is to hold the ring?* Nationalism and tribalism remain among the most potent sources of war.⁶ Dictatorships arise because at the end of the day people prefer tyranny to anarchy: they want, above all, a government that can *govern*.

Another potent cause of war is inherent in the industrial revolution, which made sense in the days when Britain was *the* workshop of the world. But 'workshops' have proliferated, and there is today, world-wide, a massive *over*-capacity for production, for example in steel, heavy machinery, shipping, aircraft, and automobiles. If you can't sell tractors, you make tanks. Without the arms trade, the heavy industry of most countries would collapse, and unemployment soar to politically intolerable levels. With the end of the Cold War, it is already happening.

Owing to Adam's inveterate inability to say No, modern technologies have been allowed to become so capital-costly that only governments and multinational corporations can use them. This is one reason why Schumacher and others have worked to develop alternative small-scale technologies appropriate to genuine human needs, including the need for 'good work' which enables each person to develop and use his own gifts in service to, and in cooperation with, others.[7]

Kohr sees bigness as itself dehumanising.

> The principal immediate cause behind both the regularly occurring outbursts of mass criminality and the accompanying moral numbness in large sections of even the most civilised societies does not seem to lie in a perverted leadership or corrupted philosophy but in a purely physical element. It is linked with frequencies and numbers, which exert an intensifying effect, and with the possession of the critical quantity of power, which has a detonating effect. At a given volume a chain reaction of brutal acts and, in due course, the appropriate condoning philosophy, will apparently result quite spontaneously.[8]

An added reason for the increase in moral numbness *especially* in 'the most civilised societies' is the increasing use of computers from primary school onwards. Like everything else in creation, the computer is ambivalent. It is a wonderful tool, but it all too easily takes over, partly because the technology itself has an obsessive fascination. Building and manipulating computer models can become an exercise in action without responsibility in a fantasy universe. Joseph Weizenbaum notes that the computer games which fill our amusement arcades are nearly all war games, accustoming the player to participation in violence without guilt.[9] Michael Shallis is also worried about the obsessiveness of computer technology and the way in which it substitutes interaction with machines for human relationships. He finds current talk of 'machines that "think"' particularly disturbing, for the anthropomorphised machine reflects a mechanised view of man.[10] In his aptly titled *The Silicon Idol*, Shallis quotes the psalmist's warning about idols:

> *They that make them are like unto them:*
> *So is every one that trusteth in them.* (Ps. 115.4–8 AV)

Neumann also sees the question of scale as central in the contemporary regression of consciousness. With the unprecedented population explosion of modern times and the drift off the land into huge cities, traditional face-to-face communities disintegrate. The majority thereupon regress to the undifferentiated 'mass man' of the collective and revert to primitive forms of behaviour, for the larger the mass, the lower the average level of consciousness, culture and morality. Increasing numbers fail to reach the standard set by the elite and are therefore regarded as inferior or anti-social.[11]

This trend is of course accelerated by the relentless 'progress' of 'labour-saving' technologies which make an ever-larger proportion of the population unemployable.[12] (What *are* employed young men to do with their energies?)

Moreover, every effort either to suppress or repress tendencies incompatible with the social ideal provokes an activation of the negative, unconscious side in both the individual and the group, as the repressed shadow accumulates in the collective unconscious. We all feed into the common pool whatever we fear to acknowledge in ourselves, and someone more vulnerable draws it out: we are in them, and they in us. There is an African tribe whose members, instead of telling you 'My brother is sick', will say 'I am sick in my brother'. Many a person diagnosed as mentally ill—or who escapes intolerable stress through drink or drugs—is in fact the vulnerable carrier of the problems of his or her family.

But in the providence of God re-collectivisation leads, by way of compensation, to a new tendency toward stability through an individuation based no longer on the conscious ego alone, but on the total psychic structure, the whole self.

The quest for perfection is abandoned as the dark shadow not only of our actual achievements but even of our ideals emerges: 'All our *righteousnesses* are as filthy rags,' says Isaiah (64.6 AV). We must leave *all* if we would follow Jesus. Above all, we must let go our cherished all-good image of ourself and stop projecting our own shadow onto others. 'Why beholdest thou the mote that is in thy brother's eye, but considerest not the beam that is in thine own eye? ... Thou hypocrite, first cast out the beam out of thine own eye; and then shalt thou see clearly to cast out the mote out of thy brother's eye' (Matthew 7.3, 5 AV).

The dark journey into the depths of self-knowledge begins. It can be, verily, a descent into hell: no more evasions; no more self-deceptions. Every eye *shall see* (Revelation 1.7)—and it is not a pretty sight. Ugly, frightening, embarrassing things emerge from the unconscious— the wild beasts and seductive enchantresses which assail the desert fathers. And there are the nameless, numinous horrors of the dark side of our pre-verbal infancy: not the blissful paradise of a loving mother's arms, but the desolation of the abandoned infant never accepted by any parental figure, the devouring hunger of one who sucks at a dry breast, the blind infantile rage that smashes things, the mindless, affectless violence of the vandal indulging a carefree sense of power. Only a strong, stable personality can confront the terrors that come from within openly, i.e. without projecting them onto somebody else. This is why in monastic tradition and practice only the mature, who have first been formed by years of community life, are allowed to undertake the solitary life of the hermit—and why such solitary contemplatives have always been regarded as the Church's spiritual front-line troops.

But the ordeal is worth the cost. The heroes of myth and legend are bidden to descend into the underworld in order to find and bring back a lost or hidden treasure. It is the pearl of great price, for which it is worth sacrificing all else (Matthew 13.45). The quest is no longer for moral perfection according to a conscious ideal, but for a *wholeness* (the word comes from the same root as 'holiness', 'health', 'healing' and 'salvation') which embraces the hitherto-rejected aspects of oneself. The stone which the builders rejected is to become the cornerstone of the new building (Psalm 118.22; Matthew 21.42; 1 Peter 2.4–8).

'Who has believed what we have heard?' says the Servant Song of Isaiah 53, telling of someone so disfigured that people avert their eyes. Yet it is through his wounds that we are healed. Our instinctive reaction to the crippled, the deformed, the mentally or physically handicapped is to turn away. They are a threat to us because their anguish and helplessness awaken the hidden anguish and helplessness and fear and anger within us. Jesus tells us (Matthew 25.31–46) that we shall be judged in the end on whether or not we have treated the alien, the sick, the poor, and the prisoner as Christ himself. But this is no mere matter of external good works done to those less fortunate than ourselves. It is a matter of so accepting and relating to such people that at the same time we recognise and welcome—as Christ himself—the alienated, sick, poor, blind, crippled person *within ourself*, imprisoned in fears, starved for affection, despised and rejected. Thus by their wounds, as by Christ's own, we can be healed.

It is this truth that is witnessed to by the L'Arche communities, founded by Jean Vanier, in which handicapped and helpers live together as equals and help each other to grow. It is a truth that is quite literally subversive, for it turns the world's values upside down ('Who can believe what we have heard?'). Those people—and those parts of ourselves—from whom we turn away with fear and loathing, are the very source of our healing, the indispensable foundation of the building up of church and society.

As long as we keep the dark side of ourselves out of sight, it exerts power over us in unpredictable and disruptive ways. Unrecognised guilt, for example, is experienced as fear by both individuals and groups. But when our dark shadow is acknowledged as our own and no longer projected onto others, healing and wholeness become possible. The last months of 1989 witnessed in Eastern Europe an astonishing example of the healing power of the collective withdrawal of projections as the Cold War faded, reality was faced, and the Berlin Wall came down.

There is a marvellous biblical image of the transforming ordeal of the encounter with the shadow in the saga of

Jacob and Esau in Genesis 32.1–33.10. Returning after years in another land, Jacob understandably fears the wrath of the brother whom he has defrauded of birthright and blessing. The crossing of water is an archetypal symbol of transformation, and at the Jabbok Ford, alone in the dark night, Jacob wrestles with his unknown Adversary—and finds that he is wrestling with the Living God. At the end of that wounding yet healing encounter Jacob is given a new identity, a new name—'Israel'—by which the people of God ever since have been known. Only then is he able to see the face of God in the face of his alienated brother, instead of his own projected hostility.

So it is with us all. Sooner or later, the disciple who perseveres finds himself at the Jabbok Ford. It is a shattering experience to recognise that the 'other side', however hostile and alien, is part of *me*: try as I may, I cannot shake it off. I must not only live *with* it; I must live *it*.

'The old idealised image of the ego has to go,' says Neumann, 'and its place is taken by a perilous insight into the ambiguity and many-sidedness of one's own nature.'[13] This fateful knowledge of good and evil banishes us for ever from the innocence of Eden. It is part of what is involved in losing one's life for Christ's sake in order to find it (Matthew 8.35).

As a collective phenomenon, nothing quite like it has ever been seen before. Never before has the 'dark side' so preoccupied all mankind as it does today: the sick, the psychopath, the addict, the cripple, the inadequate, the abnormal and the criminal absorb our attention. Ugliness, dissonance, evil and chaos force their way into art and music. The detective story and crime and horror films fascinate, and in the television news fact is often worse than fiction.

We cannot turn back the clock. Western civilisation as a whole is shifting onto a new level of consciousness which, as Neumann rightly insists, calls for a new ethic. The old perfection-seeking ethic (so necessary for the formation of responsible citizens) no longer suffices, for it has no power to transform.

A new kind of leadership is required. In the new ethic, only one who has become conscious of his own shadow and worked through his own basic moral problem is qualified to play a responsible part in the collective.

At this stage we begin to realise the full implications of loving our neighbour as ourself. 'My own shadow side is a part and a representative of the shadow side of the whole human race,' says Neumann,

> and if my shadow is anti-social and greedy, cruel and salacious, poor and miserable—if he approaches me in the form of a beggar, a negro or a wild beast—then my reconciliation with him will involve at the same time my reconciliation with the dark brother of the whole human race. This means that when I accept him and, in him, myself, I am also accepting, in his person, that whole component of the human race which—as my shadow—is 'my neighbour'. . . .
>
> It is only when I have experienced myself as dark (not as a sinner) that I shall be successful in accepting the dark ego in my neighbour; I realise my solidarity with him precisely because 'I too am dark,' *not* simply because 'I too am light.'[14]

Here is 'black theology' indeed, welcoming (as redeemed by Christ) the whole dark underside of creation: 'black is beautiful!' It is Adam coming to terms at last with the ambiguity in himself, understanding and accepting the cost of the knowledge of good-and-evil. What has to be sacrificed is innocence and unambiguous certainty.

It takes courage to make an individual appraisal of values in matters of good and evil independently of the dominant culture. All true prophets and founders of religious are heretics at first, strong individuals who dare to listen to an inner Voice. But listening to the Voice does not mean indiscriminate acceptance of everything that comes from within, let alone the unresisting acting out of every impulse: it does NOT give a blessing to the Permissive Society! We cannot skip stages. Those who exploit the acceptance of 'evil' as a means of making life easy for themselves 'are invariably people of a primitive type, who have yet to experience the values of the old ethic. It is not necessary for such people to acquire the techniques of repression, but they do need to cultivate the capacity for suppression and sacrifice, discipline and asceticism, since without this they will never achieve the ego-stability required by civilised man.'[15]

That becoming consciousness must now rank as an ethical duty is also the burden of Jung's message, discussed by Edward Edinger in *The Creation of Consciousness*.[16] Each time the conscious ego identifies itself with one of a pair of opposites, the unconscious confronts one with the other: if this new vision is accepted and not resisted, eventually one becomes able to experience both points of view simultaneously, in a sort of binocular vision. The alchemists refer to this creation of an enlarged consciousness as the birth of the Philosophers' Stone. It represents the realisation of the Self in its wholeness. It is the 'white stone with the new name written on it' of Revelation 2.17, which the risen Christ promises to the one who emerges victorious from his testing.

Those formed by the old perfection-seeking ethic understandably shrink from the ordeal, which overturns the old value-system. The new orientation partakes of the nature of the Descent into Hell and even—as in the legend of Faust and his alliance with Mephistopheles—of the pact with the Devil. The journey takes us down into 'the pagan stratum of reality underlying the Judaic and the Christian layers',[17] into the sub-verbal layer of our personality laid down in our pre-verbal infancy, before creation by the Word. There dwells the great god Pan who, with his horns and hooves, is the prototype of the Christian Devil. In Greek mythology, however, Pan is a symbol of the universe (his name means 'All') and the personification of Nature: he is playful among the nymphs and shepherds, mysterious and held in awe in woodland and mountain, but not evil in any moral sense.

The transformation of the negative was the basic preoccupation of alchemy, and the transformation of lead into gold was understood as a psychic process by the alchemists themselves. The same problem appears in different form in the Kabbalah and in Hasidism, the exuberant renewal movement which began in Eastern European Jewry in the eighteenth century.

The problem is learning to see the whole of creation as God sees it, for 'God saw everything that he had made, and behold, it was very good' (Genesis 1.31). Children can only understand the world as polarised into Goodies and Baddies, but if we are to grow up into Christ we must put away childish things. 'Love your enemies,' says Jesus to his disciples in a passage which concludes 'You must be perfect, as your heavenly Father is perfect' (Matthew 5.44–48). And the New Testament word for 'perfect' is *teleios*, which means 'complete' or 'whole'. In Neumann's new ethic, whatever leads to wholeness is good; whatever leads to splitting is evil. The Devil (*diabolos*) is a divider; God makes whole.

The new ethic is an ethic of individuation, but its collective significance is incalculable. In the old ethic, the dark side rejected by the individual accumulates in the most vulnerable sections of the group, where it contributes to outbreaks of disorder. But the truly integrated personality 'constitutes, with its stabilised structure and enlarged awareness, a rallying point and a bulwark for the collective. It is a focus of stillness amid the flux of phenomena, and the waves of collectivism and of the mass psyche will break against it in vain.' Such a person is less exposed to danger, for he has already assimilated many things from the collective unconscious which overwhelm others with horror—or compulsive attraction. 'In the catastrophes of psychic inundation which characterise periods of violent collective upheaval, such a personality forms a breakwater against mass epidemics ... and acts as a guardian and a purifier of the collective.'[18] It 'does not allow itself to be seized by the panic terror of those who are just waking to consciousness, for it has put all its terrors behind it. It is able to cope with the changing times, and has unknowingly and involuntarily become a *leader*.'[19]

Individual wrestling with collective problems can be seen in the Old Testament prophets. It is an integral part of the vocation of the disciple who perseveres, and it is profoundly redemptive. To the extent that one accepts and works through *all* that life brings, says Neumann, the individual acts as an alchemical retort in which elements from the collective are melted down and refashioned into a new synthesis. The pre-digestion of evil involved in assimilating his own shadow makes him an agent for the immunisation of the collective. An individual's shadow is bound up with that of his group, and as he digests his own evil, a bit of the collective evil is co-digested at the same time.

> In contrast to the scapegoat psychology, in which the individual eliminates his own evil by projecting it on to the weaker brethren ... we encounter the phenomenon of vicarious suffering. The individual assumes personal responsibility for part of the burden of the collective, and he decontaminates this evil by integrating it into his own inner process of transformation. If the operation is successful, it leads to an inner liberation of the collective, which in part at least is redeemed from this evil.[20]

'He was made sin for us,' says Paul concerning Jesus (2 Corinthians 5.21). And who should know so well as Paul the Pharisee the bankruptcy of the old ethic, which can neither take away sin nor make us whole, no matter how hard we try?

The New Testament singles out three Pharisees for special comment. Nicodemus comes to Jesus by night (John 3.1–22). He has gone as far as he can in the way of Torah. He has reached his 'mid-life crisis': he knows he needs to move on, but he doesn't know how; he's in the dark. To such a son of the Law, born of Torah, Jesus can speak of *re*-birth.

It is still so today. Some form of Torah is prerequisite to really hearing the New Testament Gospel. Law is the form in which love is experienced at first—at Sinai and in infancy and childhood, actual or spiritual. The 'sinless proletariat', the 'noble savage' and 'unspoilt youth' are simply those whose conscious discipleship has not yet begun, and who have not yet been brought to self-knowledge by the disciplines of the Law. Only through experience of trying to live by some sort of rule do we learn the sheer 'cussedness' of human nature *in ourselves* (see Romans 7). It is no accident that movements of Christian renewal throughout history have nearly always involved a return to the Old Testament, nor that heresies are so often rooted in its rejection.

We do not know what became of Nicodemus in the end. We do know that as a member of the Sanhedrin he had the courage to challenge the conspiracy against Jesus in the name of the Law (John 7.50–52) and that it was he, with another secret disciple, who buried the body of Jesus (John 19.38–42).

Gamaliel is revered by Jews to this day as second only to his own teacher, the great Hillel, as a master of rabbinic wisdom. He stands in the Christian record (Acts 5.34–40) as the one member of the Sanhedrin who had both the vision to perceive and the courage to pronounce the disturbing possibility that in opposing this new movement the authorities might be found fighting against God. Gamaliel, wise in the ways of God with his erring people, keeps an open mind.

His pupil Saul of Tarsus is more committed, for good and ill. A brilliant young student reading Honours Theology at the feet of Gamaliel (Acts 22.3), Saul is full of youthful zeal and impatience, certain of the righteousness of his crusade: *he* will put things right! Like many a zealot before and since, he consents to the use of violence in the service of his jealous God (Acts 7.58–8.1), but Stephen's face haunts him. Saul is above all a man of integrity, and in his heart he already knows Stephen is right. He resists seeing, redoubling his zeal in order to repress his doubt (Acts 9). But on the Damascus road (in the desert, so often the place of vision) he is blinded by the brightness of the Shekinah, in which he recognises the visible presence of the invisible God: 'Who art thou, Lord?' And the Lord identifies himself as Jesus, and in turn with his mystical Body, the Church ('whom thou persecutest').

Saul's cosmos, with its orderly structures of Pharisaic rules and certainties, collapses. And the proud, sophisticated intellectual must now humble himself to accept baptism (in Jewish practice, only for Gentile converts) and the right hand of fellowship and hospitality from the despised petit-bourgeois of the Damascus bazaar—the very people he had intended to arrest.

In due course he faces separation from family and former associates: eventually, from the synagogue itself, when finally forced to choose between loyalty to Christ's koinoinia-of-the-Spirit and loyalty to kith-and-kin and ancestral community and culture. 'Lo, we turn to the Gentiles' (Acts 13.46) is spoken by a second Abraham, going out not knowing whither he goes, blazing the trail into the Christian Dispersion.

* * *

And the Son of Man himself?

There was always a faithful remnant in Israel, especially among the rural, non-Sadducean priestly families—the 'country clergy' who took it in turn to minister in the temple of Jerusalem. Of such a family was born John the Baptist, in whom the authentic voice of prophecy was heard again in Israel after a very long silence. And John's mother, Elizabeth, and Mary, the mother of Jesus, were cousins (Luke 1.36).

Jesus's mission begins with thirty years of formation-in-community as an obscure village tradesman. From an early age he had apparently known and pondered the curious circumstances of his birth. Certainly by the age of twelve—at which a Jewish boy then became *bar-mitzvah*, a son of the Law, personally responsible for living according to Torah and fulfilling the religious obligations of a man—he had begun to grow away from his parents in pursuit of his own vocation (Luke 2.41–52).

Nazareth lies on the ridge of hills north of the historic Plain of Megiddo. Mount Tabor, an easy walk from Nazareth, offers a superb view: west toward Solomon's fortress of Megiddo (1 Kings 9.15) and Mount Carmel, scene of Elijah's confrontation with the prophets of Baal (1 Kings 18); south toward Mount Gilboa, where Saul met his death (1 Samuel 31) and Samaria, Ahab's capital (1 Kings 16.22–29). As a young man Jesus must often have climbed that 'high mountain apart' (Mark 9.2)—little more than a very large, steep hill, but it does stand apart from the range—to ponder the scenario of his people's history and destiny, spread out below. The Plain of Megiddo, the most fertile part of Palestine but geographically fated to be a battle-ground, already had a grim history. Scene of Deborah's bloody triumph over Sisera (Judges 5, 6), it had also seen the violent deaths of three kings, Joram and Ahaziah (2 Kings 9.21–28) and Josiah (2 Chronicles 35.22). Tradition associated it with Armageddon, where the Last Battle is to take place in the Day of the Lord (Zechariah 12.11; Revelation 16.18).

Thirty years was the normal age for a rabbi to commence his ministry. How was Jesus to begin? With which (if any) of the various factions among his people should he identify himself? The priestly Sadduccees of the Jerusalem Establishment? the scholarly Pharisees in their zeal for Torah? the revolutionary Zealots? the ascetic Essenes in splendid isolation at Qumran?

He decides to associate himself with the movement led by his cousin John, who has seen that the right way to prepare the way of the Lord is through the revolutionary about-face which we call repentance. Accepting John's baptism, Jesus identifies himself with all who recognise their own need for repentance: personally sinless, he takes upon himself personal responsibility for the sin of the world. (Thus the Second Adam reverses the first Adam's refusal to accept responsibility.)

Immediately there comes the Voice from heaven: 'Thou art my beloved Son, in whom I am well pleased' (Matthew 3.17; Luke 3.22; cf. Isaiah 42.1). He has made the right decision.

Then the Spirit drives him into the wilderness to wrestle with the Adversary, with his own dark Shadow, whom Mark (1.13) calls *tou satana*, '*the* satan.' In Hebrew tradition (e.g. Job 1 and 2; Zechariah 3.1) the Satan is not a proper name but the title of a functionary in the heavenly court: the Accuser, or (in modern terms) the counsel for the prosecution, at whose instigation a trial is held; or (as in canonisation proceedings) the 'devil's advocate' who puts the case against. Only later does the Satan become a metaphysical Devil;[21] originally, he represented the Loyal Opposition. Many New Testament references to him still use the definite article. 'I saw the Satan fall like lightning from heaven,' says Jesus (Luke 10.18): the day of the Accuser is over; henceforth we have in heaven not an Accuser but an Advocate (John 14.16, 15.26; Mark 13.11; Rev. 12.9–10).

Jesus is first tempted concerning his identity. This initial temptation, twice repeated, is often overlooked: '*If thou be the Son of God....*' (Matthew 4.3, 6 AV). Could be he mistaken? (It would be so much easier to go on living as an obscure village tradesman!) Why not prove it—*to himself*?

That was what Israel had wanted in the wilderness: proof (Exodus 17.1–7). And from the scriptural account of Israel in the wilderness comes the answer (Deuteronomy 8.3, 6.16): man shall not live by bread alone, but by the Word of God. Jesus will trust the word that proceeded out of the mouth of God at Jordan's stream, and will live by that, in faith—the faith that does not demand certainty but can live with doubt. Israel had not been so sure: they had tempted God, saying '*Is* the Lord among us, or no?' Israel's immemorial doubt later openly assaults Jesus: '*If thou be* the Christ, tell us plainly' (John 10.24 AV); '*If thou be* the Christ, come down from the cross ... and we will believe' (Matthew 27.40, 42). Jesus could have had the kingdoms of this world, even then, and the assurance of popular acclaim. Instead, he dies in faith, not seeing the fruit of his labours, and feeling abandoned even by God (Mark 15.34; Matthew 27.46).

Jesus is tempted concerning his vocation: what kind of authority is he to exercise, and how to do it in such a way as to enhance human freedom and not take it away?

He will not pander to the human craving for the sensational, for such manipulation of personality diminishes human freedom—the one thing God never does. Jesus does work what we (with our present knowledge) regard as miracles in order to meet human need, but he never works wonders in order to persuade men to believe (Matthew 16.1–4; Mark 8.11–13; Luke 11.29). He does not take *that* sort of 'belief' seriously; he knows human nature too well! (John 2.22–25). And he will not (in the manner of the rulers of this world) use coercion to compel people to be good.

How, then, is God's authority to be manifested in human terms?

Anyone in authority provokes resentment just by being there. It is no small part of the function of authority to *be* the butt of resentment without repaying in kind. Most anti-authoritarianism (including parental permissiveness) springs from unwillingness to shoulder this burden. I believe that Jesus saw, in the wilderness, that the only way to take away the sin of the world without compounding it is to '*take* it': to absorb the impact of whatever might be projected onto him, without fighting back. This alone can stop the never-ending see-saw, for the law that 'to every action there is an equal and opposite reaction' operates in the psychic realm as well as in physics. He knows that what he must do and say will sooner or later precipitate conflict ('I came not to bring peace, but a sword'—Matthew 10.34–36), but his way will be to accept violence, not to inflict it. And this is the way which he teaches his disciples: 'I say to you that hear, Love your enemies, do good to those who hate you, bless those who curse you, pray for those who abuse you. To him who strikes you on the cheek, offer the other also' (Luke 6.27–29; Matt. 5.38–48).

The contrast between Islam and the Christian Gospel is rooted in the different responses of Jesus and Muhammad to the same situation. Muhammad, too, experienced the opposition of religious leaders and the disaffection of his followers, and 'it looked for a moment as if he too would take the way of suffering; but then he decided to fight back on behalf of the truth. He raised his army and marched on Mecca: and that was the turning point in his career and the birth of Islam.'[22] The Qur'an says that Jesus did not actually die on the cross, but was miraculously rescued at the last moment and taken up into heaven. The presupposition is that God always vindicates his faithful servants and thus corroborates the truth of their message: that he should allow such a one to be done to death is unthinkable—especially in traditional Arab culture. It couldn't happen; therefore it didn't. (And of course where the Bible and the Qur'an disagree, for the Muslim the Qur'an is always right!)

John sees Jesus returning from the wilderness and reads in his face his decision: 'Behold the Lamb of God, who takes away the sin of the world' (John 1.29)—the willing scapegoat, on whom the Lord lays the iniquity of us all (Leviticus 16.21 AV, with Isaiah 53.5–6).

William Johnston agrees with Jung that if there is to be healing and redemption 'we must allow the barbarism that is in the unconscious to come to the surface'. We must live it, without repression, accepting and identifying with all the violence, ugliness, fear and cruelty. And,

> if it is already terrible to face and accept the hurt and injury and evil that is in our personal unconscious, how much more terrible to face the archetypal evil of the collective unconscious! How terrible to face the crisis of the afflicted and the evil of the oppressor from the dawn of human consciousness! How terrible to identify with all this!
>
> Yet I believe, with Jung, that it must be done. And I

believe that one man has done it. I believe that one man took upon himself the suffering and sin of the world. This was one who sweated blood in the garden of Gethsemane. 'For our sake he made him to be sin who knew no sin, so that in him we might become the righteousness of God' (2 Corinthians 5.21). Jesus is the lamb of God who takes away the sin of the world. But in so doing he plumbed the depth of human weakness, of human suffering, of human evil.[23]

The Eastern Orthodox icon of Easter portrays Christ's victory as the harrowing of hell: after preaching the Gospel to the departed (1 Peter 3.19, 4.6), Jesus rises through the shattered gates of hell, bringing Adam and Eve (i.e. the whole human race) back with him. The point of Christ's descent into hell is that hell is not so much a place as a state of alienation from God (2 Thessalonians 1.9)—and *when Christ goes there, it is no longer hell.*[24] Henceforth there are no depths to which we can descend where Christ is not there before us. And when our own dark shadow is brought to the healing light of Christ, it, too, loses its terrors and we are made whole.

It is at this point that the distinctively Christian point of view begins. The Old Testament looks forward to the day when God will vindicate his sovereignty against all the overwhelming evidence to the contrary. The New Testament affirms that the longed-for Day of the Lord *has dawned*, in Jesus—and the evidence is the resurrection of the body of Jesus.

'This affirmation is of great practical importance for the missionary task,' says Newbigin.

> The denial of it in various forms of gnosticism ... is very much with us today. It is present in Indian attempts to fit Jesus into the pattern of Hindu thinking as one, perhaps the supreme, illustration of the final truth for man, without disrupting the fundamentally pantheistic structure of Hindu thought. It is present in efforts to make the revelation in Christ subordinate to a general category called religion [and] in the controversy concerning demythologising.[25]

The Gospel announces that an event has taken place which is decisive for all men and for the whole of life: it is not a religious message, but the hinge of history.

> It is not the teaching of a new way of personal salvation after the manner of the Buddha. Nor is it the announcement of a theocratic kingdom in the manner of Islam. ... It is the announcement of the reign of God present and active. It sends Jesus and his disciples out on a mission which includes healing the sick and feeding the hungry as well as preaching the Good News and teaching the way of life. But it does not lead to the creation of a theocratic welfare state in Israel; it leads to rejection, crucifixion and death. And yet death is not the end: *beyond death* is resurrection and the coming of the new era of the Spirit—promise and guarantee of a new creation, of new heavens and a new earth, of the new Jerusalem.[26]

The 'fact of Christ' (his life, death and resurrection as interpreted by the apostles), like any 'fact of history', is available to us because of the judgement of contemporaries about its significance. 'It is the substance of what we mean by the "fact of Christ" that in God's long and patient wrestling with the human race, this time and place were made ready, this people was prepared, these men were chosen and trained in order that they might be the witnesses and interpreters of this unique and decisive event.'[27]

The crucial issue is the resurrection of Jesus. That men who have been dead three days do not rise from the dead was well known before the rise of modern science.

> It is no more and no less difficult to believe in the resurrection after the invention of electric light than before. ... It has never at any time been possible to fit the resurrection of Jesus into any world-view except a world-view of which it is the basis. ... The resurrection is an event which you really believe only if every world-view based on any other starting-point has collapsed. It was so for the first apostles and it has never been otherwise for any generation since.[28]

The resurrection of Jesus is a fact of history in the only

sense in which we can speak of any fact in history: it is a judgement of the evidence. 'The Christian believes that this judgement is determinative for the understanding of all history, that it is the point at which the meaning of the whole story is disclosed, and the whole story must therefore be understood from this point.'[29] In Revelation 5 it is the Lamb of God, slain and victorious, who alone is able to open the sealed book of history. In our Christian witness we are saying 'Come and look at the world from *here*'—because we believe that this point of view makes better sense of all the evidence than any other.

12

Wholeness

If only a minority of those living at any given moment in history are ready for individuality, those who have attained wholeness are the few who have found, and followed, the narrow way. For them the 'Unitive Way' of traditional Christian spirituality becomes a possibility.

The person who has said 'yes' to his own shadow, who has agreed with his adversary (Matthew 5.25), has achieved 'final integration'. This is the title of a luminous chapter in Thomas Merton's *Contemplation in a World of Action*.[1] Merton himself borrows the phrase from a book by a Persian psychoanalyst, Dr Reza Arasteh, who brings together insights from the Sufi mysticism of Persia, the humanist psychoanalysis of Erich Fromm, the existential psychotherapy of R. D. Laing and others, and the logotherapy of Viktor Frankl.

With final integration, we learn to live with ambiguity, our own and other people's and that of life itself. Our projections are withdrawn, the world is no longer polarised, the complementary opposites are re-integrated into wholeness and we are at peace. This is not the unconscious peace of the unawakened but the reflective serenity of the one whose battles have been fought and won: it is the sabbath rest of the people of God (Hebrews 4.9–10). The imperfections of our erstwhile heroes are no more disturbing to us now than the full humanity of our erstwhile villains: both exemplify the fallibility and vulnerability of the human condition. We learn to accept and to live within our own limitations, which inevitably increase with age. We seek liberation no longer from, but within, our given circumstances.

Final integration is a transcultural maturity far beyond

mere social adjustment, of which usual aim of psychiatry both Arasteh and Merton are very critical. Of what use is it to become adapted to a society which is itself sick?—a society whose acquisitive values and competitive pressures either drive people into early heart attacks and breakdowns or else leave them alienated, frustrated and bored. It is because they already perceive this that many thoughtful young people refuse to settle down as 'good citizens' and remain rebels.

Unfortunately it is easier to be a neurotic than a revolutionary. Merton notes the distinction between 'neurotic anxiety, which comes from commitment to defeat, and existential anxiety, which is the healthy pain caused by the blocking of vital energies still available for radical change'. Existential anxiety is not a sign of something wrong, but a summons to growth. Something like existential anxiety seems to have been experienced by Nicodemus (John 3) and the rich young man (Matthew 19.16–22; Mark 10.17–22). 'This anxiety is a sign of health and generates the necessary strength for psychic rebirth into a new, transcultural identity. . . . Birth on this higher level is an imperative necessity for man.'[2]

'Except a man be born again,' says Jesus to Nicodemus, 'he *cannot see* the kingdom of God'—he cannot understand what it is really about, let alone enter into it. Conventional psychotherapy is well aware that the infant must be 'born again' out of his sensual self-centredness in order to become a responsible adult. But after growing up and assuming a useful role in society, there is another birth to be undergone. In the past, this rebirth into final integration happened only to the exceptionally gifted; today the need for it is more and more widely felt, though the majority find—and are encouraged to find—innumerable ways of evading the summons.

The severe crisis which precedes final integration is not unlike the Dark Night of the Soul described by St John of the Cross in the sixteenth century. ('Anyone who chanced to fall into the Dark Night of the Soul today would, if discovered, soon find himself getting shock treatments, which would effectively take care of any further disturbing developments.'[3]) Final integration itself implies an openness to the Spirit, an emptiness, a poverty, a 'non-action' which is variously described by both Christian and non-Christian mystics. Non-action is a concept central to Asian thinking, especially in Taoism.

'The way of conscious effort is particularly important in the first part of life,' says William Johnston.[4]

> It is the way of the person who thinks, asks questions, deliberates, weighs the evidence and makes decisions. And if such a person happens to be a politician or a big businessman or a leader of some kind, then his decisions may build or destroy the lives of millions of people. But more than that: they will build or destroy his own life. For through his decisions he creates his character and makes himself.
>
> But there is another way: that of non-action, and this pertains usually (but by no means exclusively) to the second part of life. Here I am less preoccupied with doing things and more able to let things happen, less intent on making decisions and more able to allow the true decision to well up from the depths of my being.

This is the spring of living water which Jesus promises will well up within the heart of those who come to him to drink (John 4.14, 7.37-38). In John 21.18 Jesus says to Peter, 'Truly, truly I say to you, when you were young you girded yourself and walked where you would; but when you are old, you will stretch out your hands and another will gird you and carry you where you do not wish to go.' This applies to all of us. 'When we are young (continues Fr Johnston), particularly when we are young in the things of the spirit, we walk the path of conscious effort; but when we are mature we are carried along the path of non-action.'

The one who has attained final integration is no longer subject to the limitations of his own culture, but is fully catholic in the best sense. He can perceive the one truth in all its various manifestations, which he sees as complementary. 'With this view of life,' says Merton, 'he is able to bring perspective, liberty and spontaneity into the lives of others. The finally integrated man is a peacemaker, and that is why there is such a desperate need for our leaders to become such men of insight.'[5]

To the extent that we have reached this stage, the Christian ideal at last becomes realisable in a *koinonia* or fellowship in which justice, reconciliation and Christlike love even for the unlovable are manifested. Many proclaim the ideal, but few have any notion of the cost of achieving it, of integrating the *whole* of our personality—not just the reasonably mature surface bits, but also the vast unevangelised areas within which we have yet to be brought to the healing light of Christ. Strait is the gate and narrow way, and few there be who find it—or at any rate who persevere. Adam has been looking for short-cuts since the Garden of Eden, and for techniques, systems, structures, gimmicks that might save us from the tiresome necessity of being good.

Merton sees final integration as the kind of maturity which monastic life on the Benedictine pattern aims to produce, but he admits the ambiguity in practice of even that great tradition. The monastic discipline of communal service and obedience is necessary for those who have known little or no discipline of any kind, but it fosters growth only up to a certain point and within the limits imposed by adaptation to communal pattern. For those called to keep on growing beyond that point, the monastic life may eventually become as frustrating and stifling as mothering is to the adolescent. As a consequence, many leave.

This may not always be a bad thing. For many in our rootless modern world, who have never known what it is to 'belong' anywhere, the religious life may be a vitally important formative experience *for a time*, without necessarily being their life-time vocation. To make such experience more widely available on a temporary basis is a contribution which some religious communities might make at this time to the life of the church as a whole; it happens anyway in the case of novices who do not go on to profession.

Even those who remain permanently within a religious community may sometimes find themselves called, after years of living in community, to work which can better be done 'on detached service', whether an active ministry of some sort or the more contemplative life of the solitary. This, too, is not necessarily a bad thing. The Eastern Orthodox monastic tradition has always assumed that after some years in community a monk or nun may be called to the eremitical life.

What is important for all religious communities is to seek the right balance between the communal discipline essential to formation on the one hand, and on the other hand provision for the disturbing possibility of transformation and further growth. 'We have dedicated ourselves to rebirth, to growth, to final maturity and integration,' wrote Merton in the late 1960s, when the implications of the Second Vatican Council were only just beginning to be worked out. 'Monastic renewal means a reshaping of structures so that they will not only permit such growth but favour and encourage it.'[6]

Merton was of course a monk. Rosemary Haughton, writing at about the same time, wrestles with the practical problem of how the church as a whole can become the kind of fellowship in which ordinary people can be formed for transformation. A large part of the function of the church, she says, must be the creation of a language community which can provide the right kind of setting for the explosion of power that transforms.

> It isn't so easy. If you do organise and do it well, it can get to seem as if there were no need for transformation after all. . . . Why allow anything so untidy as transformation? But then the power *does* explode, in unexpected places, and usually with an inadequate language, so that people cry 'heresy' and try to screw down the lid even tighter.
>
> But if you don't organise enough, but rely on the power of the spirit to work in whatever language happens to be

around, the result is that the outbreaks are expressed in so many different languages that nobody understands what anyone else is saying, and the community-creating effect of conversation is fragmented. Also, because of the small vocabulary of these various languages, the effectiveness of conversion even on individuals is minimised.

In that case it seems that any kind of community aiming to be Christian must be an educational structure, teaching a rich and flexible language, but must also deliberately leave room for explosions which can never be entirely predictable. It sounds positively Anglican.[7]

Ideally, the Church should be a place where growth in discipleship is encouraged, where people at *all* stages of growth can find both a home and also support and guidance in working through the process of growing up into salvation (1 Peter 2.2). Is this possible?

The tension between the 'little flock' and the needs of the many is perennial. Nation-states, like ethnic and other communities, need for their cultural cohesion either a religion or a religiously held ideology. It is by no means certain that a pluralist secular society, uncommitted as a society to any particular view of truth and hence with no common basis for values, is ultimately viable. But what the New Testament offers is not religion: it is a personal faith, shared in the face-to-face *koinonia*-of-the Spirit, which challenges all religion and ideology.

The Roman Empire accurately perceived this: Christians were persecuted, not as adherents of yet another religion (that would have been tolerated) but precisely as 'atheists' who were rightly seen to be subversive of all religion. Jesus was, and is, a threat to any Establishment; so were, and are, his faithful followers. In becoming the established religion of the Empire, Christianity had to transform itself from the faith of a committed few into a religion for the masses.

As Jacques Ellul observes,[8] most people *need* a moral code and are not yet ready for the freedom and responsibility which Jesus offers. (They *talk* of freedom, but what they really want is security: freedom from want and from fear and, above all, freedom from responsibility.) Most *need* sacred places, persons and times to give meaning to the world they live in. Only those mature enough to do without the support of a homogeneous culture are able to live confidently in the de-sacralised world proclaimed by the prophets of both the Old and New Testaments—the world of the cosmopolitan city.

How can the very different conditions needed by people at different stages *all* be provided without divisiveness, especially when (with high mobility and rapid social change) so many grow up emotionally insecure? We are only just beginning to be aware of the social as well as personal consequences of the fact that increasing numbers now grow up without ever experiencing any stable family relationships. How are the spiritually deprived (who may be economically affluent) to put down the roots needed for growth? How are those who have got stuck at a particular stage to be helped to start growing again without frightening them into regression? How can those who cling to the certainties appropriate to childhood (certainties they now feel to be threatened) be helped to move on through spiritual adolescence to the adult discipleship which the New Testament takes for granted and which effective mission demands?

One thing is certain: embryo Christians cannot be magically transported from Egypt straight into the Dispersion and be expected to get on with mission. Half our frustrations are due to taking too much for granted. We long for Instant Salvation, and it is all too easy to confuse justification by faith, which we have only to accept (and which can therefore happen in an instant of time) with the long, slow process of sanctification, which is the work of a lifetime and which is unlikely to be completed this side of the grave. 'Beloved, we are God's children now; it does not yet appear what we shall be' (1 John 3.2): in Christian discipleships, the *now* and the *not yet* are always in tension.

The differing needs of those at different stages and in

differing circumstances are one reason for the persistence of different denominations. We may deplore our divisions, yet in the unity we seek there must be diversity: uniformity is not the goal. Gerald Priestland says that 'one reason why I am not really scandalised by the variety of churches is that it does offer the Christian pilgrim a series of stepping stones along which he can move; for I really see no shame in passing through several churches during a lifetime—how could I, when I have done so myself?' (He says that he 'was brought up a Public School Anglican, moved into the English Presbyterians because the sermons were better, and took to Quakerism when it occurred to me that quieter surroundings might give me a chance to hear what God, rather than Man, was trying to say.')

> I am not implying that my Presbyterian church was *better* than my Anglican church, or that the Society of Friends is *better* than either: it was simply that as I changed with age and other circumstances, the emphases of one became more meaningful to me than those of another. I am happy enough where I am for the present, but who knows where I shall end? With the Greek Orthodox, perhaps, wreathed in incense and taking the sacraments mixed together from a spoon? If we ever get one vast, uniform church—will such a pilgrim's progress be possible?[9]

What one longs for is a Christian unity where such diversity of experience would be possible without having to cross denominational boundaries: it is not the diversity, but the boundaries, that are the scandal.

Nevertheless, diversity can be very disturbing to the insecure. Great pastoral discernment and patience are needed: as with all living things, the pace of growth cannot be forced, and there are always some too vulnerable to cope with the self-knowledge needed for growth. 'We who are strong ought to bear with the failings of the weak, and not to please ourselves' (Romans 15.1).

There are diversities of gifts (1 Corinthians 12.4–11, 27–31; Ephesians 4.11–13); not all are called to be evangelists or prophets or leaders. What matters is faith and commitment to pilgrimage. And in the New Testament faith does not mean believing *that* something is true *about* Jesus, but believing *in* him—a personal relationship of trust and faithfulness. There are diversities of gifts, and this leads St Paul into that marvellous description of Christian character, the 'more excellent way' of *agapē* (1 Corinthians 13). But all are equally accepted and loved from the very start, from the moment of conception through all the stages of our pilgrimage until that day when we shall know even as we are known, when the Lord brings to light the things now hidden in darkness and the secret longings of our hearts, and everyone receives his commendation (N.B. not 'condemnation') from God (1 Corinthians 4.5).

* * *

'We are not born ourselves,' says William Johnston; 'we become ourselves. And this does not happen in a few days or weeks or months. It is the work of a lifetime, and reaches its climax only in death, which is the last stage in growth.'[10]

Death is the final detachment. Like the death which we call birth, this one, too, is a gateway to life. 'Nine months are not enough to make a man,' says Fr R. Troisfontaines, SJ. 'The first pregnancy prepares him only for bodily birth. It is the second pregnancy—the time allotted to him in this world—that prepares him for spiritual birth. The first birth destines him for death; only the second makes him enter life. We are born to die, but we die to live. Death is man's true birth: his birth to life everlasting.'[11]

'If a man keep my saying, he shall never see death' (John 8.51): if we have faithfully lived all the other deaths involved in fully human life, Jesus promises, we shall not notice this one; it will be like walking through an open door.

13
Mission and the Kingdom

Jesus preaches, and tells his disciples to preach, that 'the kingdom of God is at hand' (Mark 1.15; Matthew 10.7; Luke 10.9). What does this mean?

Shelves of books have been written about it; there must be almost as many explanations as there have been authors. Jesus himself has to resort to a wide variety of analogies and parables in order to suggest what the kingdom is like and how it manifests itself. Can our explorations shed any light?

In the Judaism of our Lord's time, God had become very remote. Even his name was unutterably holy. Some believed in a whole hierarchy of angels between God and man. We have seen that at the heart of traditional Middle Eastern kingship is availability to all one's subjects. Availability means vulnerability, and Middle Eastern rulers were, and are, very vulnerable to assassination. In the Incarnation, God made himself not only available but also vulnerable.

In Middle Eastern tradition 'kingdom' means not just sovereignty as we understand it, but the king's court, his immediate entourage, his intimates, the 'friends of the king' (1 Maccabees 2.18). To say to first-century Palestinian Jews 'the kingdom of God *is at hand*' is to say 'God is no longer remote; *he is available*; *you* can be his friend'. You may or may not enjoy 'status' (James and John had at first the wrong idea about this—Mark 10.35–45) but you will be with him, know his mind, share his purposes, drink his cup. 'I have called you friends,' says Jesus, adding 'all that I have heard from my Father I have made known to you' (John 15.15).

We cannot know how God works out his loving purpose in the majority of the human race who do not know or consciously accept Jesus as Lord and Saviour. We cannot even know precisely how he ultimately works it out in us who do. But all—of every race and culture—are to be offered the chance, here and now, to 'enter the kingdom', to be with Christ as his intimate friend in the fellowship of the Spirit, sharing his mission in loving obedience to the Father's will. ('Whoever does the will of my Father in heaven is my brother and sister and mother'—Matthew 12.50; Mark 3.35.)

Respectful, humble dialogue with those of other faiths is important, not least for what we, as well as they, may learn thereby of the unsearchable riches of Christ. But as Newbigin reminds us, 'the real point of contact between Christian and non-Christian is not in the *religion* of the non-Christian but in his *humanity*. Christ is the light that lightens every *man*.' So in our evangelism we are not trying to enrol people in our own tribal religion. 'We are not inviting strangers to come into our house. We are asking all men to come to their own home.'[1]

The one who enters the kingdom is accepted, loved, given a vocation and, in its pursuit, companionship not only with fellow disciples but also with Him whom our hearts desire above all others. The joy of 'belonging' in the court of the King is surely a great part of the joy of heaven; it is what the heavenly banquet, the marriage supper of the Lamb, is all about (Isaiah 25.6–9; Luke 14.15; Revelation 19.9).

As for those who are excluded from the presence of the Lord (2 Thessalonians 1.9)—or rather, who exclude themselves—the 'wrath of God' is simply the love of God as it is experienced by those who resist it or flee from it. God respects our free will; we cannot exclude the possibility of someone's resisting 'eternally'. But as with the infant and its mother ('in her presence is eternal life; in her absence, eternal non-being') so with our relationship to God: eternity is outside time; eternal life is not a duration but a relationship. ('This *is* eternal life, that they know thee, the only true God, and Jesus Christ whom thou has sent'—John 17.3).

Much of the motivation for mission among Western Christians in the past has arisen (and in some circles still does) from concern that individuals should be 'saved'. From lurid medieval representations of the Last Judgement to modern Bible-thumping evangelists, the concern has been with what happens to the individual after death. Scriptural warrant for this is found in Mark 16.16 (part of the later ending, not included in the original text) which says that 'he who believes and is baptised will be saved, but he who does not believe will be condemned'. But the previous verse stresses that the Gospel is to be preached to the whole creation. In the New Testament as a whole, and in the Eastern churches to this day, salvation is understood primarily as corporate and cosmic: it concerns the whole created order and the whole of human history, of which our personal history is part. In the completion of God's work in Christ, the whole creation is to be transfigured and all things restored to the unity for which they are created. Mankind is to recover the image and likeness of God, now disfigured by sin—and the whole creation is yearning to see what it will be like when we start behaving like sons of God (Romans 8.19).

Asked whether those saved will be few, Jesus simply tells the questioner to strive to enter by the narrow door (Luke 13.23–24). Curiosity about the destiny of others is not our affair (John 21.20–22). What we *are* responsible for is our own response to the call to follow Jesus in the narrow way.

That turning to Christ which we call conversion involves not merely entering into a personal relationship with him, but also commitment to the fellowship of the Church, to companionship on the Way with others who have made the same commitment. You cannot become a Christian in isolation, any more than you can become a person in isolation, for relatedness is essential to both. (You may be able to *survive* in isolation—and indeed some contemplatives choose solitude—provided that you have first been formed in community.) Christians, however isolated by circumstances, are never really alone, for we are members of the Body of Christ, of the whole Church throughout the world and beyond the veil.

The kingdom of God and the Church are not synonymous. Jesus tells his disciples to proclaim the availability of the kingdom and to demonstrate the signs of the kingdom. The mission of God, which we are called to share, is wider than the Church. (The ecumenical movement in this century has moved from seeing mission as a function of the Church to seeing the Church as a function of the mission of God.) How is the Christian disciple to recognise where God is at work?—for not everything that happens in God's world, or even in the Church, is of God. Newbigin suggests that,

> wherever he sees men being set free for responsible sonship of God; wherever he sees the growth of mutual responsibility of man for man and of people for people; wherever he sees evidence of the character of Jesus Christ being reflected in the lives of men: there he will conclude that God is at work, and that he is summoned to be God's fellow-worker, even where the Name of Christ is not acknowledged. By contrast, wherever he sees the reverse process at work, men being enslaved, mutual responsibility being denied, and the opposite of the character of Christ being produced in men: there he will recognise the work of the Devil and will know himself summoned to resist.[2]

How is the kingdom of God to be manifested among us in such a way that people begin to ask the right questions? What matters is not that we should already have attained 'perfection' (the great saints are not less but more aware of their sinfulness) but that we should be willing and able to demonstrate the way of reconciliation.

Among the messianic signs cited by Jesus from Isaiah 61.1 is that 'the poor[3] have the good news preached to them'. The liberation theologians interpret this passage politically, and in Latin America (where liberation theology began) this interpretation is cogent: most ordinary people there, and in many other parts of the world, are at a stage at which only an Old Testament gospel can be heard. Yet if Jesus had meant it that way the crowds would not have chosen Barabbas. Political saviour-figures promise heaven on earth—tomorrow, at the cost of sacrifice and suffering today. (It is the secular version of the pie-in-the-sky-when-you-die which Christians are accused of preaching.) But the Gospel is far more radical than mere political change, however urgent that may sometimes be. There are many who preach political change, and it is right that Christians should be among them. But justice is not a distinctively Christian ideal: it is (together with prudence, temperance and fortitude) one of the cardinal virtues of the pagan world, as well as being central to Torah. What Jesus has uniquely to tell the human race does not concern the things with which the kingdoms of this world are, and must be, pre-occupied. It is good news only to those who know their own spiritual poverty, who have *nothing* they can rely on but God. 'Blessed are the poor-in-spirit, for theirs *is* the kingdom of heaven' (Matthew 5.3)—*right now*: they are ready for the intimate relationship of love and trust which God offers.

'I am not sent but unto the lost sheep of the house of Israel' (Matthew 15.24 AV) refers in the first instance to lapsed Jews, who are to be recalled to their mission to be a light to the nations (Isaiah 49.6). Does it perhaps also refer to all those, of whatever race or culture, who are willing so to be prepared by discipleship to the God of Israel (who is God of all) as to know their need of him?

Jesus had to decide his priorities. He could have spent the whole of a long life healing the sick and feeding the hungry and still no more than have scratched the surface of human need, but (though these things are indeed *signs* of the kingdom) that was not how our redemption would be wrought. What was most urgent was that his disciples should be prepared for what was to come.

Ponder the gospel records: Jesus has so much to give of spiritual direction! But what most people want of him is to be fed, to be cured of their ailments, to get practical help with everyday problems. And the kingdom *is* advanced when nine lepers have their symptoms cured and are restored to society, even though (unlike the tenth) they lack the thankful faith which would complete their wholeness by bringing them into the right relationship with God (Luke 17.11–19). It takes great patience constantly to bend down to the needs of those who can understand love only in material terms (like the 'cupboard love' of small children) and are not yet ready for what he longs to give. Jesus *does* bend down: this is what the Incarnation is all about. And (as he foresees) men misunderstand. His own disciples don't get the point until on the Emmaus road he spells it out for them with chapter and verse (Luke 24.25–27). The mission of the Son of Man himself is ambiguous.

The commonest misunderstandings of the gospel are those represented by our Lord's own temptations concerning the nature of his mission. Too often in history the church has behaved as if he had yielded to them.

The first temptation concerns the human craving to be fed, to be dependent and secure. Jesus *does* feed the hungry and heal the sick. So must we, if we would share his compassion and show how those who have entered the kingdom behave. But we do not do it in order to 'convert' (that is the work of the Holy Spirit); there are to be no 'rice Christians'. We must also share his misgivings about those who ate of the loaves and were filled and then tried to take him by force and make him king (John 6.15).

The second temptation concerns the human craving for the sensational. We are urged nowadays to make better use of modern means of communication. Good. The mass media can and do inform us (for example) about famine in Ethiopia and the Sudan, floods in Bangladesh, and ecological disaster in the Amazon Valley and South East Asia. But let us be wary about adopting in the service of the gospel the means used by the persuasion industry. The manipulation of personality so widely practised in both commerce and politics is an affront to human dignity and an assault on human freedom. And it is doubtful whether a serious call to discipleship and self-sacrificing love *can* be conveyed by the mass media, which have a built-in tendency to turn everything into effortless entertainment: what they encourage is not pilgrimage but tourism.

The third temptation concerns the human passion for justice and for being in a position to enforce it—which of course means taking away some people's freedom, as the rulers of this world *must* do if human sinfulness is to be kept within bounds. But justice as a goal needs examining, for like everything in this life, it is ambiguous.

'Give sentence with me, O God, and defend my cause against the ungodly people' (Psalm 43.1): the psalmist, here seeing himself as a plaintiff seeking his rights rather than as a criminal in the dock, *wants* justice, *wants* the 'day of the vengeance of our God' foretold in Isaiah 61.2.[4] When Jesus reads this very passage in his home-town synagogue at the outset of his own mission (Luke 4.16–18), he stops reading just short of those stirring words, and we are told that the 'eyes of all in the synagogue were fixed on him'. They know exactly what he has left out, and when he spells out to those patriotic people God's love for outsiders and 'enemies', there's a riot and he's nearly lynched. Henceforth Jesus is himself an outsider, and he moves his base of operations down to the cosmopolitan frontier town of Capernaum.

Justice is a splendid standard for self-examination by 'haves'. As a battle-cry for 'have-nots' it can be a cloak for envy and revenge. Revolutionary zeal is quite as ambivalent and potentially hypocritical as patriotic zeal. It also conceals an unpalatable truth about human nature and its easy recourse to violence. For while it is true (as was observed in 1974 at a time of widespread publicity-seeking terrorism) that 'no one has yet found a way of measuring the importance of an issue except by the amount of trouble it causes', there is a deeper problem.

> The trouble with violence is not only that it works, but also that *men like it*: and there, more than anywhere, more

even than in the cruel systems that we rightly work against, is the central problem confronting theology. If the Christians had taken human nature more seriously, we might have more to say now to the warrior instinct of a generation aflame at the injustice in the world and bombing, mining, hijacking, kidnapping—the knight-errants of the late twentieth century, seeking, as we did, to hallow the violence in themselves through a cause beyond themselves. It ill becomes any one of my age, who has known the simple bliss of war as a young man, to look prune-faced at the young men now who do it again in their turn and in their way . . .

The furnace of aggression is as strongly blazing as ever in the heart of man. It is not going to go out, for it is nothing less than the fire of life itself in immaturity. If your small children *don't* show aggression, start fussing. The problem is not how to douse it but how to mature into handling it.

Moreover,

> grudge is as strong a fountain of violence as injustice. The Freudian insight into the way we tick is as important as the Marxist one. We must not imagine that every discontent has a rational economic basis, nor that the last demand has been made on love when justice is achieved. The heart of man is not that simple, and the games people play are often designed to maintain rather than to remove discontents.[5]

It is significant that in their calls for justice the Hebrew prophets address themselves to those in power: they call upon the oppressors to repent, and warn what must follow if they don't. They do not call upon the downtrodden to revolt. Their concern is not with rights but with responsibilities.

Authority must be authentic if it is to be respected. The test of the authenticity of the risen Christ is his wounds. Thomas had a right to ask to see them (John 20.24–30). They show what it cost Jesus to keep his integrity. What our witness costs us enables us, too, to speak with authority and not as the scribes.

We cannot presume to speak for those whose circumstances we do not share. They, too, must keep their integrity and accept the cost of doing so. This led the pacifist Dietrich Bonhoeffer finally to 'take the sword' (participating in the plot to assassinate Hitler) with his eyes open to the 'death by the sword' that did in fact overtake him in a Nazi prison camp. It led Camillo Torres, a gentle Roman Catholic priest in Colombia, after trying in every lawful way to bring about change in what was then one of the most oppressively unjust societies in Latin America, finally to face the realities of power in his country and to embrace the guerrilla violence in which he died.

On the other hand, there were guerrilla freedom fighters in Palestine in our Lord's day, sworn to overturn the existing order by violence. They tried very hard to make Jesus their leader (John 6.15) and in the end, as he foresaw, the people chose the gospel according to Barabbas—and perished by the sword of Rome, in AD 70 and again after Bar Kochba's revolt in AD 132–135.

Jesus has left us his comment on all this: 'You have heard that it was said, "You shall love your neighbour and hate your enemy." But *I* say to you, *Love your enemy*'— because God himself loves all men equally, just and unjust, evil and good. Christ died for *all*.

The terrible injustices in today's world understandably arouse fierce indignation. But Christians cannot simply (and self-righteously) condemn. All else apart, denunciation hardens resistance rather than encouraging repentance, for to every action there is an equal and opposite reaction. It is very tempting to localise evil in Them. But the world-view in which absolute good confronts absolute evil in total hostility is not Christian but Manichaean.[6] It is the childhood world of Goodies and Baddies, to which populations must be induced by propaganda to regress if they are to wage war. The mature know that the world is not so simple. Christ calls us to a ministry of reconciliation, which is far more difficult and costly than taking sides.[7]

(Nowhere in the world is this more painfully obvious than in Jerusalem. It is an extraordinarily difficult place in which to pray, once the initial pilgrim thrill has worn off, especially if one has friends on both sides. Each side feels itself the innocent victim of a cruel enemy; the grievances and fears on *both* sides are very real and very deep, and the more one tries to enter into them, the more one feels torn apart, caught up into the cosmic conflict which focussed once for all on the Cross but which still goes on.)

We need to ask *why* people behave unjustly. Most of those labelled 'racists' or 'oppressors' are unaware of doing wrong. They may even (like the persecuting Saul of Tarsus) fervently believe they are doing right. But they are frightened. Mostly they are very ordinary people who are unsure of their own identity, desperately insecure, and hence (behind whatever bravado they may display) terrified of anything alien, or which threatens change or loss or the opening of the eyes of the blind. Understanding this is part of 'loving our enemy', and only love can cast out fear. Learning to do it is vital to our own spiritual growth, for the mote in our brother's eye is as nothing to the beam in our own. The real enemy is always within.

The kingdom of God is also within—or it is nowhere. Peace and justice are *fruits* of the kingdom: they appear on earth when, where, and to the extent that God's authority is freely accepted in the hearts of men and women. Like happiness, they are by-products which cannot be had by pursuing them for their own sakes. Nor can true peace and justice be imposed upon the unwilling by force. Though in a sinful world force is very often needed, what is imposed by force is always less than truly just or peaceful. But where men and women willingly enter the kingdom of God and accept his sovereignty, there peace and justice and the other signs of the kingdom become visible.

'Behold, *now* is the day of salvation,' says St Paul (2 Corinthians 6.2), who goes on to describe the paradoxes of discipleship and mission:

> We are treated as impostors, and yet are true; as unknown, and yet well known; as dying, and behold we live; as

punished and yet not killed; as sorrowful, yet always rejoicing; as poor, yet making many rich; as having nothing, and yet possessing everything.

The whole of our Christian discipleship lies within the paradox of the *now* and the *not yet*.

It has been so from the beginning, from that first exuberant Pentecostal proclamation that the Day of the Lord had at last been inaugurated in the death and resurrection of Jesus. 'Love's redeeming work is done,' as the Easter hymn says, yet it soon became clear to the infant Church that that work was manifestly *not* yet completed. This growing tension can be seen in Acts and in the epistles. It led some to speculate that there might be a *Second* Coming of Christ. Perhaps it is significant that this development coincided with the expansion of the Church from its original Semitic base among people steeped in Hebrew/Aramaic thought-forms to include increasing numbers who thought in Greek (with its past, present and future tenses) and knew nothing of the Hebrew perfect.

The shift from awareness of the risen Christ present and active among us *now* to the idea of an absentee Christ who will return later is discussed by John Robinson in *Jesus and His Coming*.[8] He points out that biblical statements about the end of the world, like those about the beginning, are mythological, i.e. metaphysics written as history: they 'are not to be taken as predictions; they represent, rather, theological convictions about the ultimate vindication of God in Christ.'

All New Testament imagery concerning 'the end' is borrowed from Jewish apocalyptic expectations about the coming of the Messiah. The New Testament word *parousia*, usually translated 'coming', also means 'presence'. And Jesus himself is primarily concerned with the impact of his presence *now*: 'This *is* the judgement, that light is come into the world, and man prefer darkness' (John 3.19).

* * *

'Is it not selfish to engage on an inner journey and to

encourage others to do so in a world where millions starve through the greed of others and where our very existence as a human race is threatened by nuclear weapons?' asked Gerard Hughes in 1978. But, he continued, 'it was Einstein who said, "The release of atomic power has changed everything except our way of thinking, and thus we are being driven unarmed towards a catastrophe. ... The solution to this problem lies in the heart of humankind." It is our thinking and perceiving which must change.'[9]

In the same year William Johnston, commenting on the Second Vatican Council's call for communal conversion, observed that while such a conversion did take place at Pentecost, 'I believe that such Pentecosts are rare. More often the salvation of the group is achieved through the conversion of the few. "For the sake of ten I will not destroy it" (Genesis 19.32). There are people who, following Jesus in Gethsemane, take upon themselves the suffering of the world. We need such people today.'[10]

Such are the seed of Abraham, in whom all nations of the earth are to be blessed.

'I begin to see (said Fr Hughes in 1985) that the real battle is not in working to change the structure of the Church and of society, but in struggling to change the structure of my own psyche. This may sound very individualistic and selfish, but the only thing we can change is ourselves, for the only power that can bring creative change is God. I cannot domesticate God, I cannot tell him what to do, no matter how noble the cause: all I can do is let his glory through in me, let God be God in my own life.'[11]

The personal pilgrimage of discipleship is prerequisite to effective mission. There is a great spiritual hunger. People today, says John Main, are looking for the fruits of the Spirit: peace, liberty, joy, the freedom and power to love. 'Above all, they are seeking the courage and strength to *be* . . .'

> If today's pilgrims are not turning to the Christian tradition, it must surely be due in large part to their failing to see among us enough men and women who have evidently been restored to themselves and who therefore know the urgency and personal dimension of the pilgrimage. ... Unless the Word has inspired us to leave self behind and to follow the light of Christ as his intimate disciples, then we cannot hand on the gospel with its living, true and effective power.[12]

It is not enough, therefore, to call people to engage in evangelism without also acquainting them with the implications and the cost thereof. For evangelism is not an external 'good work' to be promoted by publicity campaigns. It is the witness we make when asked to give a reason for the hope that is in us (1 Peter 3.15).

> We are called to be a people of knowledge who have become full persons. In answering this call we are empowered to answer the call of our contemporaries for guidance, inspiration, above all for *knowledge of the Truth*. Much of our reluctance to answer this call in the past has been due to a reluctance to make the complete commitment of ourselves to the pilgrimage.

We have given lip service to the gospel, but it has not yet noticeably affected our way of life. It is not enough to proclaim the Good News of what God *has done*; people need to see what he *is doing* now. Being convinced of the historicity of the Gospel events is not usually the first step on the road to belief. The resurrection of Christ is a necessary antecedent to the living Christ, but it is to the living Christ that people respond, in the power of the Spirit—not to the historical fact that Jesus was raised two thousand years ago.

Thoughtful people, weary of propaganda and hypocrisy, are hungry for authenticity. 'The Church is called to teach,' said John Main,

> and at no other time has its teaching been more urgently needed. It does not teach through committees or organisa-

tions or reports and manifestoes. It teaches through persons. It teaches through us—provided that we have seriously set foot on the pilgrimage and begun our personal encounter with the Master.

If we have not, then what we *are* will speak so loudly that people will not be able to hear what we say.

NOTES

Chapter 1: Poetry and Paradox
1. Princeton University Press, 1969.
2. Oxford University Press, 1962.
3. *The Finality of Christ* (SCM Press, 1969), p. 62.
4. See Cyprian Smith, *The Way of Paradox*: Spiritual Life as Taught by Meister Eckhart. Darton, Longman & Todd, 1987.
5. Gill & Macmillan, 1979, p. 63–65.
6. *The Subversion of Christianity* (Wm. B. Eerdmans, 1986), p. 44. Emphasis his.
7. See Russell Stannard, *Science and the Renewal of Belief* (SCM Press, 1982), Chapter 18, 'The Place of Paradox in Science and Belief.'

Chapter 2: Discipleship and Mission
1. C. S. Lewis describes thus a turning point in his long agnostic struggle against faith: 'Early in 1926, the hardest boiled of all the atheists I ever knew sat in my room on the other side of the fire and remarked that the evidence for the historicity of the Gospels was really surprisingly good. "Rum thing," he went on. "All that stuff of Frazer's about the Dying God. Rum thing. It almost looks as if it had really happened once."' (*Surprised by Joy*, Geoffrey Bles, 1955, p. 211.)
2. *The Mirror Mind:* Spirituality and Transformation (Collins, 1981), p. 90.
3. Adam is not a proper name but (like the Greek *anthropos*) an inclusive term for the whole human race.
4. In his epoch-making book *Personal Knowledge:* Towards a Post-Critical Philosophy (Routledge & Kegan Paul, 1958) Michael Polanyi points out that the modern scientific community is itself a 'faith community'.
5. Russell Stannard, head of the physics department at the Open University, discusses this at length in *Science and the Renewal of Belief* (SCM Press, 1982) and especially in *Grounds for Reasonable Belief* (Scottish Academic Press, 1989). See also Angela Tilby, *Science and the Soul: New Cosmology, the Self, and God* (SPCK, 1992).
6. *The Turning Point:* Science, Society and the Rising Culture (Wildwood House, 1982), p. 83. In *The Tao of Physics* (Fontana, 1976) Capra explores the similarity between the world-view of modern physics and that of mystics of all ages.
7. Russell Stannard explores this line of thinking in Chapter 16 of *Grounds for Reasonable Belief*, pointing out the similarity to the way modern physicists think of the realities of the physical world.
8. St Paul discusses this theme in Romans 8.19–21, Epheisans 1.9–10 and Colossians 1.15–20.
9. I.e. Isaiah 40–55.
10. In *The Primal Vision* (SCM Press, 1963), pp. 121–123, John V. Taylor describes the impact of this discovery upon the traditional African world-view.
11. The Hebrew word *radah* in Genesis 1.26 (in the post-exilic preface to the

book) is usually translated 'have dominion'. But in Genesis 2.15 (from a pre-exilic tradition) *abad* ('to till') means that Adam is to serve the garden as its servant or slave, and *shamar* ('to keep it') implies watchful care and preservation. The notion that the rest of creation exists solely for our benefit and that we may exploit it as we please has indeed been widespread among Christians, and has led to Christianity's being blamed for the ecological mess the world is in today. But that notion comes not so much from the Bible as from Aristotle (whose influence on medieval scholasticism was enormous) and from Descartes at the beginning of the 17th century. In the context of the Bible as a whole it is clear that what Adam is given is a stewardship for which he is responsible to God. See Tim Cooper, *Green Christianity* (Hodder & Stoughton, 1990) and John V. Taylor, *Enough is Enough* (SCM Press, 1975).
12. John Lawrence, *Take Hold of Change* (SPCK, 1975), p. 22.
13. P. 35.
14. See, for example, Neil Postman, *Amusing Ourselves to Death:* Public Discourse in the Age of Show Business (Methuen, 1987).
15. Shabbir Akhtar, *The Light in the Enlightenment:* Christianity and the Secular Heritage (Grey Seal Books, 1990), p. 174.
16. There is growing concern even among computer experts about the effect of the ever-increasing use of computers on the users themselves, on human relationships generally, and on our perception of the world around us. See, for example, Joseph Weizenbaum (Professor of Computer Science at the Massachusett's Institute of Technology), *Computer Power and Human Reason:* From Judgement to Calculation (Penguin, 1984) and Michael Shallis (of Oxford University), *The Silicon Idol:* The Micro Revolution and Its Social Implications (Oxford University Press, 1984).
17. St Paul Publications, 1982.
18. *Op. cit.*, p. 245.
19. On this subject, see Jacques Ellul, *The Subversion of Christianity*, Chapter 5, 'The Influence of Islam'.

Chapter 3: The Growth of Consciousness
1. John 6.14–15 and 18.36 with Matthew 26.51–54. Jesus is the Greek form of Joshua; both mean 'saviour'.
2. The essence of prophecy in the Old Testament is not fore-telling (prediction) but forth-telling (proclamation).
3. Matthew 13.14–15, Mark 4.12, Luke 8.10, John 12.20, Acts 28.26–27, Romans 11.8.
4. Jeremiah 5.21, Ezekiel 3.4–11.
5. *The Origins and History of Consciousness*, p. xvi.
6. Geoffrey Chapman, 1967, pp. 7–8, 11, 134–136.
7. That Jesus tells us (Matthew 18.3–4, Mark 10.15, Luke 18.17) that we must become as little children if we would enter the kingdom is a call to childlike humility and receptivity, not to childish self-centredness and self-will.
8. *In Search of a Way:* Two Journeys of Spiritual Discovery (Darton, Longman & Todd, 2nd edition of 1986), pp. viii–ix.
9. William Johnston follows this approach in his illuminating study of mysticism and religon, *The Inner Eye of Love* (Collins, 1978).

10. See his *Letters to Contemplatives*, Fount, 1991.

Chapter 4: In the Beginning
1. There is growing evidence that the mother's emotional states, especially anxiety and distress, are shared with the foetus from quite early in pregnancy. See Frank Lake, *Tight Corners in Pastoral Counselling* (Darton, Longman & Todd, 1981).
2. *Op. cit.*, p. 6.
3. Have we not all watched a baby sucking its own toe? We did it ourselves, once.
4. Psalm 74.13–14, Job 41.1, Isaiah 27.1 and 51.9.
5. Neumann, *op. cit.*, p. 15.
6. In *The Pursuit of the Millennium* (Paladin, 1970) Norman Cohn demonstrates the close link which has always existed between mysticism and anarchic revolution.
7. Literally 'healthy-minded' (1 Timothy 1.10, 1 Timothy 4.3).
8. *Op. cit.*, p. 113.
9. Quoted by Robert Jungk in *Brighter Than a Thousand Suns* (Penguin, 1960), p. 266.
10. Exodus 16.2–3, Numbers 11.1–6, 14.1–4.

Chapter 5: Exodus
1. See Frank Lake, *op. cit.*, pp. 17–20, 147–148.
2. *Op. cit.*, p. 104.
3. *The Inner Eye of Love*, p. 50.
4. *The Mirror Mind*, p. 39. The same point is made by Russell Stannard in *Grounds for Reasonable Belief*, p. 233.
5. The Hebrew community in Egypt numbered no more than could be served by two midwives, whose names we know (Exodus 1.15).
6. Judaism was a proselytising religion all around the Mediterranean before and after the time of Jesus; it proved so attractive to the Roman upper classes that in AD 41 the emperor Claudius forbade the Jews to proselytise and in 49 actually expelled them from Rome for a time (Acts 18.2). In the eighth century the Khazar kingdom of the Caucasus—a 'third force' between Byzantium and the Arabs—opted for Judaism rather than for either Christianity or Islam, and there is considerable evidence that much of Eastern European Jewry (especially in Poland, Russia and Lithuania) is descended from Khazars who migrated into Eastern Europe after the fall of their own empire in the thirteenth century. See Arthur Koestler, *The Thirteenth Tribe: The Khazar Empire and Its Heritage* (Hutchinson, 1976).
7. See Gabriel Hebert, *When Israel Came Out of Egypt* (SCM Press, 1961), Chapter V, 'The Christian Exodus'.

Chapter 6: The All-provider
1. This may sometimes be a factor in both male homosexuality and the correspondingly man-centred 'hysteric' personality in women. (Lesbianism, with its attachment to women, has different roots.) See Frank Lake, *op. cit.*, ch. 10, 'Pastoral Understanding of Homosexuality'.
2. William Johnston explores this theme in depth in *The Mysticism of the Cloud of Unknowing* (Anthony Clarke, 1978).

3. See Johnston, *The Mirror Mind*, pp. 161-163.
4. *Op. cit.*, pp. 165-166.
5. Dunstan McKee of the Society of the Sacred Mission, 'Sexuality in the Celibate Life', in the *SSM* magazine for May 1989.
6. For a compassionate discussion of this whole subject, including fetishism, paedophilia and homosexuality, see Anthony Storr, *Sexual Deviation* (Penguin, 1964).
7. There may well be an inherited predisposition, though with psychological characteristics—as distinct from purely physical ones such as colour of eyes or hair—it is impossible to know to what extent the inheritance is transmitted genetically and to what extent by psychic contagion. There is also likely to have been emotional damage suffered at or soon after birth, or even before.
8. 'The Curative Community', in *Man in Community* (World Council of Churches, 1966), pp. 252-254.
9. Anthony Storr gives a very good short account of how analytical psychotherapy heals wounded people in Chapter 12 of *Sexual Deviation*. But such a healing relationship can also happen in other ways.
10. *The Glass of Vision* (Dacre Press, 1948), p. 109.
11. See Chapter XI of Anthony Storr, *The Integrity of the Personality* (Heinemann, 1960 and Penguin). This invaluable little book is the best discussion I know in layman's language of the whole process of growing up to maturity and of the ways in which things can go wrong.
12. This, according to Mircea Eliade, is the original purpose of city walls: they are a magic defence before they are a military, defining, in the midst of a chaos peopled with demons, a space that is organised, made cosmic, provided with a centre. See *Patterns in Comparative Religion* (Sheed & Ward, 1958), p. 371.
13. The tetragrammation YHWH is more accurately translated 'I will be what I will be', since the verb 'to be' in Hebrew has no present tense. This revelation of God's overwhelming transcendence became *so* holy in Jewish tradition that (since well before the time of Jesus) no observant Jew ever pronounces it, using instead *Adonai*, 'the Lord'. To this day, no one really knows how YHWH was pronounced.
14. See David Pryce-Jones, *The Closed Circle:* An Interpretation of the Arabs (Paladin, 1990), especially Ch. 2, 'Shame and Honour'. Hence the futility of attempts by the United Nations, and by Western governments generally, to deal with the immemorial conflicts of the Balkans and the Middle East on the basis of appeals to Security Council resolutions or international law.

Chapter 7: Conquest

1. See Anthony Storr, *Human Aggression* (Penguin, 1968), which sets the insights of Konrad Lorenz's *On Aggression* (Methuen, 1966) and Robert Ardrey's *The Territorial Imperative* (Collins, 1967) in a larger context. Erich Neumann also discusses the topic in *Depth Psychology and a New Ethic* (Hodder & Stoughton, 1969), Chapter III, 'Stages of Ethical Development'.
2. Modern anthropology has confirmed Peter Kropotkin's refutation of the idea that Darwin's 'survival of the fittest' necessitates universal competiton.

In his book *Mutual Aid* (first published in 1902 and reissued in 1987 by Freedom Press) Kropotkin points out that the most successful species are those whose members have learned to cooperate.
3. *The Road to Daybreak* (Darton, Longman & Todd, 1988). p. 65.
4. Viktor Frankl, a Jewish psychiatrist who lost all but one of his family in the Holocaust and himself survived three years in Auschwitz, learnt there that those who survived were the ones who, like himself, had found meaning in their suffering. Interpreting *logos* as 'meaning', he later used his experience as the basis for a new way of healing sick souls. See *Man's Search for Meaning:* An Introduction to Logotherapy (Hodder & Stoughton, 1964).
5. Eve is 'the mother of all living' (Genesis 3.20), and that she is said (Genesis 2.21–22) to be made out of Adam's rib is true to our infant experience: the first thing to emerge out of our undifferentiated perception of the humanity around us *is* our mother and, in particular, our mother's breast.
6. 'Even in woman, consciousness has a masculine character. The correlation "consciousness-light-day" and "unconsciousness-darkness-night" holds true regardless of sex. ... Consciousness as such is masculine even in women, just as unconsciousness is feminine in men.' Neumann, *The Origins and History of Consciousness*, p. 42.
7. *Fire Upon the Earth* (Edinburgh House, 1958), p. 4.
8. Neumann, *op. cit.*, p. 123.
9. Anton Wessels, *Images of Jesus* (SCM Press, 1990), pp. 68–69.
10. Kathleen Kenyon, *The Bible and Recent Archaeology* (British Museum, revised edition of 1987) pp. 72–75. The same must have been true at Ai (the name means 'ruins'), which had been destroyed a thousand years before and not rebuilt (*ibid.*, p. 71). The account of its capture in Joshua 8 fits the geography very exactly except for the numbers (thirty thousand) said to have been involved, which must in fact have been more like a couple of platoons than a regiment: no way could you conceal five thousand men in that little ravine! The narrator must have known this (Ai is only a half-day's walk from Jerusalem), but factual accuracy is not his concern.
11. Neumann, *Depth Psychology and a New Ethic* (Hodder & Stoughton, 1969), pp. 104–105.
12. *Sexual Deviation*, p. 31.
13. John Lane The Bodley Head, 1946, pp. 390–391.
14. Those who dislike the term 'priestess' should ask themselves *why* they dislike it. You do not get rid of the unpleasant connotations of a *thing* by refusing to call it by its proper name.

Chapter 8: The Promised Land
1. Faber, 1967, p. 76.
2. *Depth Psychology and a New Ethic*, p. 38.
3. *Ibid.*, p. 50.
4. *Ibid.*, p. 52.
5. Oxford University Press, 1967.
6. See Giovanni Garbini, *History and Ideology in Ancient Israel* (SCM, 1988), pp. 31–32.

Chapter 9: Exile
1. Freud is an admirable example of his own theories. See Erich Fromm,

Sigmund Freud's Mission (Allen & Unwin, 1959) and Helen Walker Puner, *Freud: His Life and His Mind* (Dell Books, 1959).
2. In *Memories, Dreams, Reflections* (Collins & Routledge & and Kegan Paul, 1963, p. 154) Jung recounts how on the long sea voyage to a conference in American he and Freud were engaged in mutual dream analysis. At one point Jung asked Freud for some further associations and Freud refused, saying that to disclose these would 'risk his authority'. ('At that moment he lost it altogether,' adds Jung.)
3. Jung describes the occasion when Freud confided this to him—*ibid.*, pp. 147ff.
4. His autobiographical *Memories, Dreams, Reflections* will repay thoughtful reading. Jung's insights are only just beginning to penetrate popular consciousness, since they are to a large extent scattered through a mass of clinical and literary material in the many thick volumes of his *Complete Works*. Jung's only effort to reach the general public was his last work, *Man and His Symbols* (Aldus, 1964). More recently Laurens van der Post, one of Jung's closest friends in his later years, has explored the deeper significance of his contribution in *Jung and the Story of Our Time* (Pantheon, 1975).
5. See *Memories, Dreams, Reflections*, pp. 231, 255.
6. Karl Popper vividely described this in his contribution to a discussion of Russell's philosophy in *The Listener* for 14 May 1970.
7. Most notable of these are Melanie Klein and W. R. D. Fairbairn. Their pioneering work is ably summarised in Harry Guntrip's *Personality Structure and Human Interaction* (Hogarth Press, 1961), which traces the development of psychodynamic theory from Freud onward. At a more popular level, see D. W. Winnicott, *The Child, the Family and the Outside World* (Penguin, 1954). The writings of R. D. Laing shed much light on this, especially *The Divided Self:* An Existential Study in Sanity and Madness (Penguin, 1965). The most exhaustive treatment of this theme is to be found in the massive original version of Frank Lake's *Clinical Theology* (Darton, Longman & Todd, 1966), of which an abridged version edited by Martin H. Yeomans was published in 1986. Lake links the schizoid state with the *Angst* of writers as varied as Job, Kierkegaard, Simone Weil, and also with the crucifixion of Christ.
8. The scripts were published by Penguin in 1967. The plays were rebroadcast in 1989.
9. Flamingo (Fontana), 1989.
10. 'The Second Coming', in *The Collected Poems of W. B. Yeats*, Macmillan, 1924.
11. *Bomb Culture* (Paladin, 1970), pp. 18–19.
12. *Ibid.*, p. 105.
13. *Ibid.*, pp. 23–24.
14. Not to be confused with individua*lism*.
15. *The Eternal Now* (SCM, 1963), p. 11.
16. Longmans, 1967.

Chapter 10: Dispersion
1. *The Origins and History of Consciousness*, p. 335.

2. Methuen, 1948 (reprinted in *A Matter of Eternity* by Mowbrays in 1973), pp. 12, 16.
3. SPCK, 1972.
4. *Op. cit.*, pp. 7–9.
5. *Ibid.*, p. 10.
6. *Ibid.*, p. 77.
7. Michael Joseph, 1968, Chapter 3, 'Urban Jungles'. The whole book is illuminating. More light is shed on the problems arising with the break-up of traditional societies in his *Parasitism and Subversion:* The Case of Latin America (Pantheon, 1966).
8. For a fascinating discussion of this whole subject, see G. J. Whitrow, *Time in History:* Views of Time from Prehistory to the Present Day (Oxford University Press, 1988).
9. Quoted by Paul Clifford, then President of the Selly Oak Colleges in Birmingham, at a USPG conference in 1971.
10. *Honest Religion for Secular Man* (SCM Press, 1966).
11. Newbign, *op. cit.*, p. 23.
12. *A Faith for This One World?* (SCM Press, 1961), pp. 18–19.
13. Hence the modern Western domination of what was once an Arab empire stretching from Gibraltar to Baghdad has been not only politically humiliating but also theologically incomprehensible—until in 1973 the discovery of the power of the oil in the Muslim heartlands led to a recovery of nerve and a resurgence of Islam.
14. The other great foundation of Western civilisation, the Greek culture which reached its zenith in fifth-century BC Athens, evolved at about the same time as the Judaism of the second temple. (Pericles was contemporary with Nehemiah.) But Athenian society rested on slave labour, and Athenian education was élitist and more concerned with physical training and music than with literature. The moral education of the many was provided by the Greek dramatists, whose plays were watched—almost as a religious ceremony—by huge crowds.
15. See Jacob Neusner, *Torah Through the Ages:* A Short History of Judaism (SCM Prss, 1990), pp. 28, 32.
16. *A Hidden Revolution:* The Pharisees' Search for the Kingdom Within (Abingdon, 1978), pp. 302–303.
17. *Ibid.*, p. 301.
18. Faber & Faber, 1949, pp. 31–33.
19. Basil the Great, Gregory of Nyssa and Gregory of Nazianzus.
20. John A. T. Robinson argues very persuasively that the entire process could have, and probably did, take place *before* the fall of Jerusalem. See his *Redating the New Testament*, SCM Press, 1976.
21. Benedict Viviano of the École Biblique et Archéologique in Jerusalem makes a strong case for this, though he dates the Gospel later, after AD 70.
22. *Jews and Christians:* The Myth of a Common Tradition (SCM Press, 1991), p. 11.
23. The Christian community in Jerusalem had held liturgical celebrations at the site of the Empty Tomb until AD 66, and recent Armenian excavations under the Church of the Resurrection indicate that Latin-speaking pilgrims came there at least as early as the second century.
24. See Robinson, *op. cit.*, Chapter IX.

25. Criticism of Israeli government policies does not, however, constitute 'anti-semitism'. Once a people are in a position of power, they are responsible for how they exercise it, and can no longer credibly claim the 'innocent victim' role.
26. The *birkat ha-minim* or benediction against the 'heretics', which was introduced into the Eighteen Benedictions *ca* AD 85–90, apparently concerned who was competent to lead synagogue services as precentor and did not constitute expulsion from the community. In any case, 'deviationism' was, and is, assessed by Jews more by failure to keep the Law in practice than by unorthodox belief. See John A. T. Robinson's 1984 Bampton Lectures, *The Priority of John* (SCM Press, 1985), p. 72–77.

Chapter 11: The Stone that the Builders Rejected
1. *Foolishness to the Greeks*, p. 116.
2. *Op. cit.*, p. 35.
3. *The Age of Plenty:* A Christian View (St Andrews Press, 1974), p. 21. The theme is developed at length in Schumacher's classic *Small Is Beautiful:* A Study of Economics as if People Mattered (Blond & Briggs, 1973; Abacus, 1978).
4. Published by Routledge in 1957, reissued in Wales in 1974, and republished by Routledge in 1986 with a foreword by Ivan Illich.
5. *Op. cit.*, p. xxiii–xxiv.
6. It was the never-ending tribal warfare of 19th-century Africa which led David Livingstone in 1857 to articulate the Victorian sense of the civilising misision of Western Christendom in his celebrated call for 'Christianity and commerce' (i.e. legitimate commerce, to replace the slave trade) for Africa.
7. See E. F. Schumacher, *Good Work* (Jonathan Cape, 1979), pp. 3–4.
8. *Op. cit.*, p. 33.
9. *Computer Power and Human Reason*, pp. xv–xvii.
10. *The Silicon Idol*, p. 4.
11. *Depth Psychology and a New Ethic*, p. 70.
12. Shallis observes that 'the effect of new technologies on labour has been understood for centuries, and there are many recorded cases of machines being broken up by employees or by local government officers in medieval times; even the Roman emperor Vespasian opposed water power for fear that it would create unemployment. The assumption that the Luddites were wrong is part of modern prejudice.' *Op. cit.*, p. 129.
13. *Op. cit*, pp. 79, 82, 93.
14. *Ibid.*, p. 95.
15. *Ibid.*, p. 111.
16. Subtitled 'Jung's Myth for Modern Man' (Inner City Books, Toronto, 1984).
17. Neumann, *op. cit.*, p. 116.
18. *Ibid.*, pp. 128–129.
19. Quoted by Neumann from Jung's Complete Works, Vol. 17, p. 179.
20. Neumann, *op. cit.*, p. 130.
21. Russell Stannard suggests that the Devil has come into being because human beings choose to relate, not to God, but to that which is not God

(the 'negative pole to God') and which exists only in our relatedness to it (just as electrons exist only in their relatedness to each other). One can, he suggests, imagine a fallen angel, created in and for relationship to God, setting himself up as a rival focus for human relatedness, thereby severing his own relatedness to God and becoming dependent for his existence on human beings who choose to relate to him rather than to God. See *Grounds for Reasonable Belief*, pp. 242–243.

But the Devil is a master of the *non sequitur*: his cleverest ploy is to persuade us that, because he does not really exist (but is 'only' a projection of our imagination) therefore we need not take him seriously. Imagination is one of the most potent forces there is, for good or ill.
22. John V. Taylor, *The Go-Between God* (SCM, 1972), p. 188.
23. *The Mirror Mind*, pp. 149–150.
24. For 'hell' the New Testament sometimes uses *hades*, the Greek equivalent of *she'ōl*. But Jesus more often speaks of *Gehenna*, which is simply the Jerusalem rubbish tip in the Hinnom valley, 'where their worm dieth not and the fire is not quenched' (Mark 9.48, quoting Isaiah 66.24). The image is of the eternal destruction (non-being) of that which is alienated from God.
25. *A Faith for This One World?* pp. 62–63.
26. *The Finality of Christ* (SCM, 1969), pp. 48–49.
27. *Ibid.*, p. 76.
28. *Honest Religion for Secular Man*, pp. 53–54.
29. *The Finality of Christ*, p. 85.

Chapter 12: Wholeness
1. George Allen & Unwin, 1971.
2. *Op. cit.*, pp. 209–210.
3. *Ibid.*, p. 214.
4. *The Inner Eye of Love*, p. 100.
5. *Op. cit.*, p. 212.
6. *Ibid.*, p. 216.
7. *The Transformation of Man*, pp. 149–150.
8. *Op. cit.*, Chapter III, 'Desacralization and Sacralization'; Chapter IV, 'Moralism'; and Chapter VIII, 'The Heart of the Problem'.
9. *Who Needs the Church?* (St Andrew Press, 1983), pp. 3, 13–14.
10. *The Mirror Mind*, p. 30.
11. 'The Mystery of Death', in *Theology* for October 1970.

Chapter 13: Mission and the Kingdom
1. *A Faith for This One World?* p. 65.
2. *The Finality of Christ*, pp. 83–84.
3. The New Testament word translated as 'poor' in these passages and in Matthew 5.3 is *ptōchos*, which means literally 'shy', 'timid', 'fearful'; the corresponding word in Isaiah 61.1, *anav*, means 'humble' or 'meek'. In their primary meaning, both words have a psychological or spiritual rather than an economic connotation, referring to the diffident and the inadequate—who, because they cannot hope to compete with the confident and the capable, become also economically poor.

4. Amos (5.18–20) warned those who desired the Day of the Lord that it would be darkness and not light, but his warning went largely unheeded.
5. Peter Wyld in *This World and the Next* (USPG annual report, 1974), pp. 43–44. Emphasis mine.
6. Manichaeism was a Gnostic sect which originated in Persia in the third century. St Augustine was a Manichaean before he became a Christian.
7. The whole question of Christian participation in violence is explored in depth by Jacques Ellul in his book *Violence* (SCM Press, 1970).
8. SCM Press, 1957 and 1979. This is still, after 35 years, the most illuminating treatment of this subject. The quotation is from p. 10.
9. *In Search of a Way*, p. xi.
10. *The Inner Eye of Love*, p. 151.
11. *God of Surprises* (Darton, Longman & Todd, 1985), p. 154.
12. *Community of Love* (Darton, Longman & Todd, 1990), pp. 16–18.

INDEX

Abelard, 78, 109
Abraham, 1, 9, 13, 15, 42, 46, 65, 74, 86, 103, 113, 115, 127, 146, 174
accidie, 37
Achan, 116
Adam, 7, 9–11, 64, 67, 95, 135, 141, 147, 151, 157, 178n., 181n.
adolescence, 22, 62, 71, 91–92, 96–98, 102, 104, 157, 160
Aelred of Rievaulx, 109
agapē, 55, 89, 94–95, 162
aggression, 11, 25, 49, 54, 61, 79, 101, 134, 170
Ai, 81, 181n.
Akhtar, Shabbir, 178n.
alchemy, 34, 142–143
ambiguity, ambivalence, 9–10, 11, 25, 56, 67, 79, 91, 94–96, 97, 133, 136, 141, 154, 157, 168, 169
Ambrose, St., 108
Amos, 47, 110, 186n.
Andreski, Stanislav, 112
Antiochus Epiphanes, 120, 126
anti-semitism, 129, 131, 184n.
anxiety, 9, 11, 26, 40, 49, 66, 95, 98, 155
apartheid, 129
Aquinas, Thomas, St., 110
Arabs, 59, 127–128, 130, 179n., 180n., 183n.
Arasteh, Reza, 154–155
archetypal images, 6, 22, 32, 57, 72, 105, 140
Ardrey, Robert, 180n.
Aristotle, 107, 115, 123, 134, 178n.
ascetical theology, ix
astrology, 34
atheists, 94, 159, 177n.
Athens, 15, 183n.

Augustine, St., 62, 108, 186n.
Auschwitz, 98, 181n.
authority, 59, 66, 68, 73, 93, 149, 170, 172
    breakdown of, 31, 85, 100

Baal, 45, 60, 68–69, 147
Babel, Tower of, 12
Babylon, 33, 103, 111, 119, 127
Bacon, Francis, 31
baptism, 18, 42, 146, 147
Barabbas, 128, 167, 171
Bar Kochba, 171
Bedouin, the, 46, 83
Beersheba, 1, 81
'belonging', 29, 75, 77, 85, 91, 122, 164
Benedictines, 82, 157
Berkeley, George, 48
Bernard of Clairvaux, St., 4, 109
Bethlehem, 1, 81
birth, 21, 32, 39–43, 48, 57, 104, 162
Bonhoeffer, Dietrich, 171
Buber, Martin, 22
Buddhism, 18, 35, 41, 117
Bühlmann, Walbert, 17, 18
Bunyan, John, 102
Byzantine Greeks, 127
Byzantium, 107, 110, 179n.

Caesarea, 125
Cain, 11
Canaan, 42, 44, 46, 70, 103
Canaanites, 44, 68, 83, 127
Cappadocian Fathers, 123
Capra, Fritjof, 7, 177n.
Casserley, J. V. Langmead, 123
Cassian, John, 108
celibacy, 50–52

certainty, 10, 13, 35, 89, 125, 133, 148
  loss of, 31, 92, 98, 101, 102, 141, 160
  vs. faith, 24
charismatic movement, 25, 28, 58
childhood, 21, 22, 32, 62, 68, 79, 88–89, 92, 96, 98, 104, 145, 171
Chosen People, the, 17, 60, 70, 84, 129
Chrétien de Troyes, 109
Christ, vii, 11, 14, 17, 18, 19, 24, 35, 62, 72, 73, 74, 109, 115, 116, 139, 143, 151, 157, 164, 170, 171, 175, 182n. See also Jesus.
Christendom, 15, 19, 31, 66, 73, 77, 88, 89, 98, 107, 111, 128, 184n.
Church, the, 13, 18, 22, 67, 72, 76, 109, 113, 125, 130, 131, 146, 159, 166, 174–175
Cicero, 108
Cistercians, 109
Claudius, emperor, 179n.
Clement of Alexandria, 17, 19
Cohn, Norman, 179n.
communal world, 10, 87
community, communities, 32, 75ff., 85, 87–89, 103, 112, 129
Communism, 79
competition, 61–62, 155, 180n.
complementarity, 5, 132, 154, 156
computers, influence of, 16, 36, 136, 178n.
consciousness, growth of, vii, ix, 10, 16, 22, 25, 32, 58, 61, 70, 79, 89, 114, 142, 150
  collective, 20, 81, 92, 106
  personal, 22, 28–29, 39–40, 53, 58, 110, 122
Constantine, emperor, 13, 21
conversion, 10, 19, 24, 159, 165, 174
Cooper, Tim, 178n.
Cornelius, baptism of, 129
Covenant, the 20, 44, 60, 78, 81, 83, 86, 119

creation, 2, 7–8, 9, 15, 30, 32–33, 40, 42, 63, 111, 118, 134, 141–142, 165, 178n.
Crusades, the, 87, 128
Cyrus, 111, 119

Dark Night of the Soul, 25, 155
David, 2, 21, 43, 83–84, 87
Day of the Lord, 47, 151, 169, 173, 186n.
death, 11, 22, 23, 39, 104, 162
  spiritual, 36, 37
depression, 26, 55, 62, 98
depth psychology, ix, 2, 22, 34, 181n.
Descartes, René, 31, 105, 132, 178n.
detribalisation, 103
Deuteronomy, 44, 45, 70, 86, 112, 118–119
Devil, the, 78, 99, 142, 143, 148, 184n.
discipleship, vii, ix, 2, 13, 21, 22, 28–29, 65, 73, 97, 104, 122, 145, 159, 160, 167, 172–173, 174–175
Dispersion, the, 46, 110, 118–119, 127, 146, 160
dragon-slaying, 34, 69–70, 74, 92
drug sub-culture, 101

Easter, 14, 47, 151
Easter Vigil, 42
Ecclesiastes, Book of, 15
Eckhart, Meister, 3, 177n.
Edinger, Edward, 142
Egypt, vii, 20, 31, 33, 37, 42–46, 58, 81, 117, 160
Einstein, Albert, 174
Eliade, Mircea, 180n.
Elijah, 60, 91, 110, 147
Ellul, Jacques, 4, 13, 134, 159, 178n., 186n.
Engels, Friedrich, 79, 88
Enlightenment, the, 31, 133, 178n.
entropy, 25, 50
eros, 49–50, 53–55, 94
Essenes, the, 47, 83, 147

INDEX

Establishment, the, 97, 117, 159
   in Jerusalem, 125, 129, 131, 147
eternal life, 49, 164
Eucharist, the, 47, 73
evangelism, vii, 19, 103, 164, 175
Eve, 11, 66–67, 74, 151, 181n.
evolution, 21, 23, 25, 34, 50, 132
Exile, the, 31, 44, 46, 86, 91ff., 104, 110–112, 117–118
existentialism, 2, 30, 94, 98
Exodus, the, 20, 42–47, 58, 69, 70, 81, 86, 104, 115
Ezekiel, 21, 112
Ezra, 83, 118, 119

Fairbairn, W. R. D., 182n.
Farrer, Austin, 57
father-figure, the, 55, 65–68, 72, 74, 93
Faust legend, the, 142
fellowship, 13, 157, 158
   of the Spirit, 13, 76, 159, 164
final integration, 154–156
Fison, J. E., 68
formation, 19, 20, 23–24, 60, 75, 80, 82, 88, 89, 119, 146, 158, 165
Frankl, Victor, 154, 181n.
freedom, human, 11, 12, 13, 37, 98, 100, 149, 159–160, 174
French Revolution, the, 98, 106, 133
Freud, Sigmund, 11, 25, 50, 93, 97, 170, 181n.
Fromm, Erich, 154, 181n.
fundamentalism, religious, 133

Galilee, the, 47, 127
Gamaliel, 145
Garbini, Giovanni, 181n.
Garstang, John, 70
Genesis 1–11, 2, 6, 8–9, 11, 30, 32, 39, 64, 67, 94, 177n.
Gentiles, the, 19, 22, 111, 120, 125, 126, 128, 130, 146
George, St., 70, 74
Gethsemane, 151, 174

ghetto, the, 87, 129
Gideon, 44
Gnosticism, 22, 36, 151
'God-fearers', 14, 120
Gospel, the, 14, 16, 18, 20, 30, 88, 103, 110, 112, 117, 120, 144, 152, 167, 175
Great Mother, the, 22, 34, 58, 65–69, 74, 78
Greek philosophy, 17, 19, 107, 123

Habiru, the, 46, 83
Hadrian, emperor, 126
Hasidism, 22, 58, 143
Haughton, Rosemary, 23–24, 158
Hebert, Gabriel, 3, 179n.
Hebrew language, the 6, 65, 114, 173, 177–178n., 180n.
Hebrews, the 8, 43–46, 78, 81, 82, 114
Hebron, 81, 83, 127
hell, 56, 95, 185n.
   descent into, 138, 142, 151
Hellenism, 120–121
Herod the Great, 125
Hezekiah, 83, 86
Hinduism, 18, 35, 40, 113, 116, 151
Hiroshima, 98
history, vii, ix, 3, 6, 14, 15, 17, 18, 20, 44, 47, 113–116, 117, 123, 126, 152, 165, 173, 175
Hoch, Erna, 53–55
Holocaust, the, 128, 181n.
Holy Spirit: see Spirit, Holy
Hooker, Roger, 18
Hosea, 42, 72, 109, 110
Hughes, Gerard, 27, 174
human rights, 59, 102, 113, 116, 132

'Illuminative Way', the, 122
Incarnation, the, 17, 18, 20, 74, 163, 168
India, 18, 40, 53, 77, 87, 115
individualism, 29, 133, 182n.

individuality, 10, 29, 76, 92, 94, 102, 105–106, 110, 111–112, 122, 132, 133, 154
individuation, 137, 143
industrialisation, problems arising from, 86, 102, 135
infancy, 11, 16, 22, 26, 34, 41, 49–50, 55, 58, 64, 68, 74, 91, 96, 138, 142, 145
innocence, loss of, 96, 100, 143
integration, 22, 24, 26, 48, 50, 75, 105, 154–156
Isaiah, 8, 21, 110, 122
Isaiah, Second, 9, 31, 46, 69, 110, 111, 120, 138
Islam, 18, 19, 66, 77, 87, 88, 113, 116, 124, 128, 133, 150, 152, 178n., 179n.
Israel, ancient, 9, 17, 19, 46, 64, 73, 81, 88, 89, 91, 107, 110, 112, 116, 130, 140, 146, 148, 181n.
  in Egypt, 20, 37, 42
  northern kingdom of, 81, 86
Israel, modern State of, 83, 130, 184n.

Jacob, 9, 31, 44
  and Esau, 1, 140
Jebusites, 2, 83
Jeremiah, 11, 15, 21, 46, 103, 112
Jericho, 70, 81
Jeroboam, 84, 86
Jerusalem, vii, ix, 1, 2, 14, 21, 31, 42, 44, 45, 47, 83, 84, 103, 111, 118, 120, 125, 127, 129, 171, 181n.
Jesus, 3, 4, 5, 13, 17, 18, 21, 42, 47, 68, 72, 96, 110, 116, 118, 129, 130, 143, 144, 146, 148–149, 150, 155, 162, 163, 164, 165, 167, 168, 169, 171, 173, 174. See also Christ.
Jethro, 42
Jews, the, 14, 31, 46, 47, 83, 106, 110, 118, 121, 122, 125, 126, 129, 145, 163, 167, 179n.

jihad, the, 87
Job, 32, 33, 116, 182n.
John the Baptist, St., 17, 47, 146, 147, 150
John the Evangelist, St., 15, 163
John of the Cross, St., 4, 109, 155
Johnston, William, viii, 4, 6, 29, 41, 51, 150, 156, 162, 174, 178n., 179n.
Joshua, 20, 44, 70–71, 81
Joshua, Book of, 44, 70, 119
Josiah, 83, 86–87, 147
Judaea, 47, 127
Judaism, 6, 11, 22, 88, 119–121, 124, 125–128, 131, 163, 179n.
Judah, southern kingdom of, 81, 86
judgement, 14, 15, 88, 173
  Day of, 130, 165
Judges, Book of, 70, 82
Jung, C. G., ix, 6, 34, 93, 94, 142, 150, 182n.
justice, vii, 10, 21, 157, 167–170, 172

Kabbalah, the, 22, 143
Kelly, Herbert, viii, 8
Kenyon, Kathleen, 70, 181n.
Khazars, the, 179n.
Kierkegaard, Søren, 182n.
Kingdom of God, the, 47, 163ff., 168, 172
Klein, Melanie, 182n.
Koestler, Arthur, 179n.
Kohr, Leopold, 134–136
koinonia, 76–77, 87, 89, 129, 130, 146, 157, 159
Kropotkin, Peter, 180n.

Laing, R. D., 154, 182n.
Lake, Frank, 179n., 182n.
language, disintegration of, 15–16, 31
Law, the, 3, 21, 24, 120–121, 126, 143, 145, 146
law, 13, 59, 62, 100, 131, 144
Lawrence, John, 178n.

Lewis, C. S., 72, 114, 177n.
liberation theology, 20, 69, 166
literacy, 106–107, 110, 117
Livingstone, David, 184n.
Lorenz, Konrad, 180n.

Maccabees, the, 83, 120, 122
Main, John, 174–175
Manichaeism, 171, 186n.
Marx, Karl, 79, 88
Marxism, 79, 86, 94, 134, 170
Mary, the mother of Jesus, 146
'mass man', 37, 137
mass media, 16, 31, 37, 98, 106, 168
Maurice, F. D., 16
McKee, Dunstan, 180n.
meaning, 6, 15, 16, 30, 32, 64, 98, 114, 126, 153, 181n.
meaninglessness, 15, 39, 102
Megiddo, Plain of, 147
Merton, Thomas, 154–158
Messiah, the, 14, 83, 95, 173
messianic signs, 14, 87, 95, 166
Mishnah, the, 59, 124. See also: oral law
mission, vii, 8–9, 13, 20, 103, 112, 116, 120, 126, 160, 164ff., 169, 175
monasticism, 13, 138, 157, 158
monotheism, 9, 111–112, 124, 128
moral theology, 78, 93
morality, 25, 31, 60, 99, 101
Morgan, Lewis Henry, 79, 88
Morris, Colin, 108
Moses, 20, 42–43, 46, 58, 59, 81, 84, 86, 104, 117, 121
mother-figure, the, 48–49, 55–56, 62, 68, 89, 93. See also: Great Mother
Muhammad, 18, 116, 124, 150
Murry, John Middleton, 75
Muslims, 11, 15, 89, 107, 113, 125, 127–128, 130, 150
mysticism, 29, 34–35, 41, 50, 110
myth, 6, 11, 30, 32–33, 64, 94, 173

nationalism, 76, 126, 135
Nazareth, 147
Nehemiah, 44, 83, 118, 120, 183n.
Neumann, Erich, 2, 22, 32, 36, 39, 70, 79, 105, 136, 140, 144, 180n., 184n.
Neusner, Jacob, 126, 183n.
Newbigin, Lesslie, viii, 3, 115, 133, 151, 164, 166, 183n.
New Covenant, the, 15, 47, 112
New Testament, the, 13, 15, 18, 19, 20, 22, 65, 72, 88, 110, 113, 116, 118, 125, 130, 144, 148, 151, 159, 162, 165, 173
Newton, Isaac, 7, 31, 34
Niblett, W. R., 75
Nicodemus, 144–145, 155
Nietzsche, Friedrich, 94
nihilism, 98, 99
Noah, 12, 45
Nouwen, Henri, 62
Nuttall, Jeff, 99–101

Oedipus myth, the, 10
Old Testament, the, 2, 8, 15, 17, 20, 34, 35, 65, 72, 109, 110, 116, 118, 122, 130, 131, 145, 151, 167
Opie, Iona and Peter, 81
Oppenheimer, J. R., 36
oral law, the 59, 121, 124, 126
Origen, 109, 125
original sin, 11, 18, 96

Palestine, 46, 70, 125, 126, 147, 171
Palestinians, 127–128, 130
pantheism, 33, 151
paradox, 2–5, 172–173, 177n.
Passover, the, 1, 46, 47, 87, 126
patience, importance of learning, 64
Paul, St., 4, 10–12, 15, 18, 24, 47, 50, 67, 117, 125, 130, 144, 162, 172, 177n. See also: Saul of Tarsus
peer group, the, 29, 79, 97, 111, 113
Pelagius, 11, 96
Pella, 125

Pentateuch, the, 59, 86, 119, 120–121, 124
Pentecost, Day of, 1, 12, 14, 15, 47, 128, 173, 174
people of God, the, vii, ix, 65, 130, 140
perfection, quest for, 122, 137, 138
  ideal of, 10, 11, 23, 40
personal relationships, 16, 22, 41, 55, 62, 92, 97, 105, 109, 122, 165
personality, vii, 18, 26, 58, 61, 64, 71, 123–124, 138, 149
Peter, St., 14–15, 24, 47, 156
Pharisees, the, 12, 83, 121, 124, 131, 144–145, 147
philia, 54–55, 87, 105
Philistines, 127
pilgrimage, vii, 13, 24, 27, 115, 162, 169, 174–175
Plato, 40, 122
Polanyi, Michael, 177n.
polarisation into opposites, 10, 33, 39–40, 79, 132, 133, 143, 154
polytheism, 78, 122
Post, Laurens van der, 182n.
Postman, Neil, 178n.
prayer, growth in, 28–29
Priestland, Gerald, 161
projection, 9, 27–28, 37, 57, 80, 129, 132, 137, 139, 149, 154, 184n
Promised Land, the 20, 47, 70, 81, 84, 88, 89, 103, 112
prophets, 7, 15, 21, 47, 83, 91, 114, 124, 141, 144, 160, 170
Pryce-Jones, David, 180n.
puberty, 54, 71, 77, 92, 100
'Purgative Way', the, 89
Puritan ethic, the, 131

Qmran, 147
Qur'an, the, 125, 150

rabbis, 21, 119, 126, 131, 147
racism, 80, 87, 129, 172
rationalism, 3, 133

rationality, 15, 26, 65, 99, 105, 133
reconciliation, 59, 80, 141, 157, 166, 171
Reformation, Protestant, the, 77, 90, 106, 128
regression, 15, 22, 26, 35, 37, 40–41, 50, 68, 98, 120, 125, 128, 133, 136, 160
Renaissance, the 106–107, 110
repression, 11, 25, 79, 93, 142, 150
responsibility, 9, 13, 15, 29, 37, 65–67, 159–160, 170
  communal, 88, 133
  personal, 21, 29, 53, 60, 91, 98, 104, 105, 110–112, 116, 144, 147
resurrection of the body, 121–122
  of Christ, 47, 151–152, 173, 175
Rivkin, Ellis, 121, 124
Robinson, John A. T., 173, 183n., 184n.
Russell, Bertrand, 94

sabbath, the, 118, 154
Sadducees, the, 47, 83, 122, 124, 131, 147
salvation, 4, 9, 12, 15, 18, 126, 138, 152, 159, 160, 165, 172, 174
Samaria, 81, 86, 147
Samuel, 82
Sanhedrin, the, 126, 128, 145
Sartre, Jean-Paul, 2, 56, 94
Satan, the, 133, 148
Saul, king, 43, 82, 147
  of Tarsus, 77, 124, 145–146, 172
Sayers, Dorothy L., 107
scapegoats, 10, 37, 52, 54, 87, 103, 129, 132, 144, 150
scholasticism, 110
Schumacher, E. F., 134, 135, 184n.
science, modern, 7, 31, 40, 115, 152
Seabrook, Jeremy, 103
Second Coming of Christ, 173
self-knowledge, 10, 25, 57, 58, 109, 138, 145, 161
Septuagint, the, 121

sexuality, 25–26, 50–53, 62, 66, 71, 79, 93
shadow, the, 9–10, 12, 79–80, 129, 131, 132, 133, 137–141, 144, 148, 151, 154
Shallis, Michael, 136, 178n., 184n.
Shechem, 44, 81, 120
Shiloh, 82
sin, 15, 18, 20, 23, 26, 49, 78, 89, 95, 109, 144, 147, 149, 151, 165
Sinai, the, 1, 43, 59, 81, 115, 121, 145
singular, philosophical problem of the, 122–123
Socrates, 122
solitude, 58, 63, 97, 102, 165
Solomon, 21, 81, 83–84, 86, 87, 109, 147
Song of Songs, the, 109
Sophia, 34, 73
speech, power of, 9, 63–64
Spirit, Holy, 5, 14, 19, 28, 58, 108, 148, 152, 164, 168, 174–175
Stannard, Russell, 177n., 179n., 184n.
Stephen, St, 125, 145
Stoics, 108, 122
Storr, Anthony, viii, 71, 97, 180n.
suffering, 11, 15, 18, 21, 64, 79, 95, 116–117, 144, 151, 167
suppression, 79, 142
synagogue, the, 14–15, 117–119, 125, 127, 131, 146, 169
syncretism, 19, 84

Talmud, the, 5, 110, 124, 127
Taoism, 156
Taylor, John V., 41, 178n., 185n.
technological society, the, 17, 36–37, 115
television, influence of, 16
Tell el-Amarna letters, 46
temple at Jerusalem, the, 84, 118, 125, 126

Temple, William, 7, 75
temptation of Jesus, 74, 96, 149, 168–169
Tilby, Angela, 177n.
Tillich, Paul, 98, 102
Torah, the, 43, 59, 70, 117, 120–121, 126, 127, 144, 146, 147, 157
Transfiguration, the, 24, 47
transformation, 23–24, 26, 48, 88, 91, 104, 139–140, 142–143, 158
tribal cultures, 48, 59, 71, 77, 81, 92, 112
tribalism, 9, 76, 86, 128, 133, 135
Trinity, doctrine of the, 7
Troisfontaines, R. J., 162

unconscious, the, 6, 22, 25, 32–33, 35, 36, 58, 93, 138, 150
   collective, 132, 137, 143, 150
'Unitive Way', the, 154
USPG, viii, ix, 18, 186n.

Vanier, Jean, 139
Vespasian, emperor, 126, 184n.
violence, 37, 59, 61, 64, 70, 101, 130, 136, 138, 145, 149, 150, 169–171, 186n.

weaning, 22, 48, 61–62, 104
Weil, Simone, 182n.
Weizenbaum, Joseph, 136, 178n.
Wessels, Anton, 181n.
Western civilisation, 31, 37, 92, 99, 133, 140
Whitrow, G. J., 183n.
wholeness, 9, 35, 52, 138–139, 142–143, 154ff; 168
wilderness, the, 20, 24, 42, 58, 148, 150
William of St Thierry, 109
Winnicott, D. W., 182
wisdom, 16, 21, 57, 73, 93, 103, 131, 145
womb, the, 21, 33–34, 40, 42, 48, 96, 104

Wyld, Peter, 186n.
'wrath of God', the, 164

xenophobia, 87

Yahweh, 44, 60, 68–69, 72, 78, 83, 84, 87, 109, 111
Yavneh, 126
Yeats, William Butler, 99, 182n.

Yohanan ben Zakkai, 125–126

Zealots, the, 47, 124, 128, 147
Zechariah, 120
Zen, 4
Zion, Mount, 83, 103
Zionists, 70, 128, 130
Zohar, the, 109